FIGHTING WARS, PLANNING FOR PEACE

THE STORY OF

GEORGE C. MARSHALL

Lee Gimpel

MORGAN
REYNOLDS
PUBLISHING
Greensboro, North Carolina

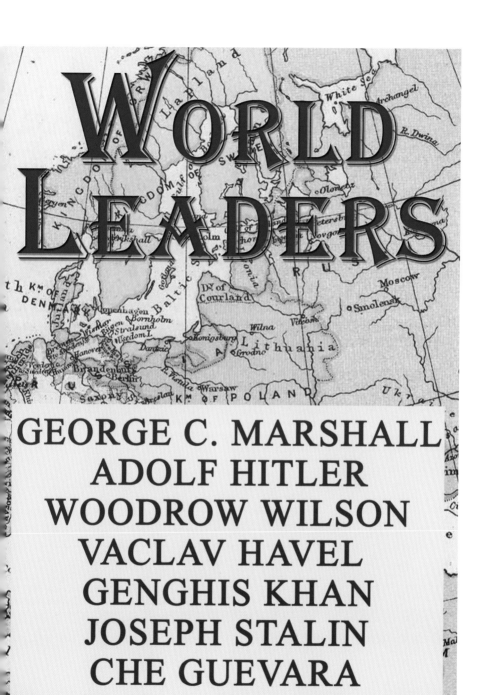

WORLD LEADERS

GEORGE C. MARSHALL
ADOLF HITLER
WOODROW WILSON
VACLAV HAVEL
GENGHIS KHAN
JOSEPH STALIN
CHE GUEVARA

FIGHTING WARS, PLANNING FOR PEACE:
THE STORY OF GEORGE C. MARSHALL

Copyright © 2005 by Lee Gimpel

Library of Congress Cataloging-in-Publication Data

Gimpel, Lee, 1976-
    Fighting wars, planning for peace : the story of George C. Marshall /
        Lee Gimpel. p. cm.
Includes bibliographical references and index.
    ISBN-13: 978-1-931798-66-2 (library binding : alk. paper)
    ISBN-10: 1-931798-66-4 (library binding : alk. paper)
    1. Marshall, George C. (George Catlett), 1880-1959—Juvenile literature.
2. Generals—United States—Biography—Juvenile literature. 3. Statesmen—
United States—Biography—Juvenile literature. 4. United States.
Army—Biography—Juvenile literature. I. Title.
    E745.M37G56 2005
    973.918'092—dc22

                        2005005037

Printed in the United States of America
First Edition

Dedication

*In memory of my grandmother, Eleanor Gimpel,
one of the Greatest Generation*

Acknowledgements

*Thanks to both the George C. Marshall Foundation
and the George C. Marshall International Center
at Dodona Manor*

CONTENTS

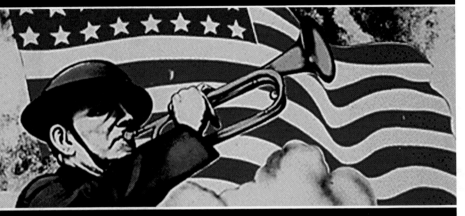

ONE

FROM UNIONTOWN TO VMI

One of George Marshall's ancestors was John Marshall, the second and, many argue, most important chief justice of the United States Supreme Court. Marshall was understandably proud of this ancestor, and of others who had served the country in different ways. But it made him uncomfortable when people mentioned his lineage. George Catlett Marshall was both a confident and a humble man. He took immense pride in the work he did, earning universal respect from superiors and subordinates alike, yet he was willing to stay behind the lines while other generals won glory in battle. Still, a lifetime of hard work and patience would win Marshall his own place in history.

Opposite: General George C. Marshall. *(Courtesy of the National Portrait Gallery, Smithsonian Institution / Art Resource.)*

Marshall was born on December 31, 1880, in Uniontown, Pennsylvania, the youngest of three children of George Catlett Sr. and Laura Bradford Marshall. Although his family was living in Pennsylvania when he was born, the Marshalls traced their roots back to a prominent Virginia family. Marshall's immediate family lacked the acclaim of some of their better-known relatives, but his father was a successful businessman who was involved in supplying coke, the coal fuel used in making steel. George Marshall Sr. later made a name for himself in local politics.

As a result of his father's successful business, George Marshall's family lived comfortably. However, in 1890 George Marshall Sr. sold many of his business interests, took the substantial proceeds, and invested it in property in Virginia. For a few months, it seemed as if the Marshalls

Uniontown, Pennsylvania, at the end of the nineteenth century. *(Library of Congress)*

George Marshall Sr. *(Courtesy of the George C. Marshall Foundation.)*

were approaching the well-to-do status of some of the more famous industrialists of the time—Carnegie, Mellon, Rockefeller—but this illusion ended quickly. The property company turned out to be a disaster, and the family was nearly ruined. The Marshalls struggled financially; Laura Marshall even had to ask for food scraps to prepare meals.

Yet the shift in the family's fortunes didn't significantly change young George, other than to instill in him an appreciation for thrifty living. Like others his age, the blue-eyed boy with the snub nose enjoyed hearing about the daring deeds of the Wild West, not far removed from his own childhood. He avidly read adventure stories and begged for tales of his father's brief service as a soldier during the Civil War, which had ended only fifteen years before he was born. Though his father was a stern man, in later years George would fondly recall the time they spent together. Sometimes this meant going out hunting or fishing. Other times his father would delve into a favorite subject: the local history of Uniontown and its surroundings. These talks would include the old National Road—the country's first major highway—which ran by the Marshalls' two-story brick home, as well as stories about Fort Necessity. It was there, not far from Uniontown, that General Edward Braddock was killed in battle, not long after he and his troops had tried to aid a young lieutenant colonel named George Washington at the outbreak of the French and Indian Wars.

George Sr. also liked to relate the Marshall family history. George Jr., however, was bored by the deeds of his forbearers and recalled, "My father was so keen in family interests that I was rather sensitive about it and I was embarrassed by his keenness. I thought that the continual harping on the name of John Marshall was kind of poor business. It was about time for somebody else to swim for the family."

George did not share his father's interest in genealogy, though he did enjoy learning about history. But outside of history, George did not excel in school. He was, at times, ashamed of his academic weakness. He was not very good at sports, either. George was very much a typical turn-of-the-century boy with an enter-

George *(far right)*, with his sister Marie and brother Stuart in 1884. *(Courtesy of the George C. Marshall Foundation.)*

prising spirit. Called "Flicker" by his close friends for his habit of flicking his hair from his forehead, Marshall engaged in a number of boyish schemes, most of them with his best friend, Andy Thompson. The two set up a stand to sell licorice water, presented circus-like performances with their pets, and opened a bar in George's basement selling his father's root beer—until Mr. Marshall caught the boys and put an end to it.

On another occasion, George and Andy started a ferry service. Using a small raft, they carried girls across a shallow stream as a shortcut to school. For this they collected a small fee. One day, when the ferry was halfway across the stream, the girls mutinied and declared that they were not going to pay the fare. Not one to be taken advantage of, George decided that he would get even with the girls: he pulled the plug from the raft and scuttled the small ship, getting all of the passengers wet.

George Sr. was generally tolerant of his son's escapades, perhaps because they showed he had the makings of a businessman. His mother had a sense of humor about her son's antics. She would sometimes laugh when she heard of George's pranks, such as the time George and Andy tried their hand at illegal cockfighting, or when they played at being highwaymen and held up local farmers on the road with a BB gun. Of his mother's influence on his behavior, Marshall would recall, "I told

Laura Bradford Marshall circa 1905. *(Courtesy of the George C. Marshall Foundation.)*

her everything I did, and she never corrected me. Because if I told her, I realized it was wrong and there was no use telling me again that it was wrong."

Throughout his life, George remained close to his sister, Marie, but not his brother, Stuart, whom he felt was favored by their father. Despite the coolness that existed between the two brothers, George decided to follow Stuart's lead when it came time for him to choose a university and a career path.

George attended the Virginia Military Institute, as his brother had done. Although VMI was a military academy, it lacked the prestige and credentials of the United States Military Academy at West Point, the army's official institution of higher learning. An education at West Point would have been free, but the cost of a year at VMI was $400—a lot of money in those days, particularly given George Sr.'s up-and-down finances. Still, it was unlikely that Marshall would have been accepted to West Point. Not only were his grades not good enough, but he had also injured his elbow and it had not properly healed—something that could disqualify him as physically unfit. Finally, and perhaps most importantly, he would have needed a recommendation from one of the Republican senators from Pennsylvania at a time when his father was a prominent member of the Democratic Party.

Before he left for school, George Jr. overheard Stuart talking to his mother, objecting to George attending VMI: "He was trying to persuade her not to let me go because he thought I would disgrace the family name.

Well, that made more impression on me than all the instructors, parental pressure, or anything else. I decided then and there that I was going to wipe his eye."

George had gotten into the school partly based on his family's reputation. Certainly, his admission had not been guaranteed by his less-than-stellar academics, and his transition was not an easy one. Though his was a prominent and respected Virginia family name and he had relatives who had attended the school, coming from Pennsylvania meant he stuck out like a sore thumb. At the time—only a few decades after the Civil War—VMI was a bastion of Southern manners and culture. The headmaster himself had fought against Union troops. Not surprisingly, Marshall's classmates were suspicious of the pug-faced boy who talked with a different accent.

On top of the fact that he was a Yankee in a Southern school, Marshall was also an awkward young man who had trouble with the various drills and marches that students were put through. First-year students at military academies often had to endure a year of mistreatment from the older students. At VMI the new students were called rats. Their initiation included doing chores such as cleaning older students' rooms. The rats were also subjected to serious hazing that sometimes threatened their safety. Sticking out among his fellow rats, Marshall was subjected to an unfair amount of mistreatment. Once, an older student set a bayonet knife on the floor, with the point up and told Marshall to crouch over it.

The Virginia Military Institute in Lexington, where Marshall attended school from 1897 to 1901. *(Library of Congress)*

As the minutes ticked by and Marshall's muscles grew weak from the effort of crouching over the blade, he refused to show any sign of weakness in front of the older student. Eventually his legs gave out and he sliced himself (though not too seriously) on the blade. Marshall was stoic about such treatment: "It was part of the business and the only thing to do was to accept it as best you could."

Conduct that endangered younger students was technically against the rules, but when asked about the incident by administrators, Marshall wouldn't elaborate on his injury. This was good news for his tormentors because if he had told on them, they likely would have been severely punished or even thrown out of school. For this, Marshall won the respect not only of the older students but also his own classmates. Soon Marshall had adjusted to life at VMI, learned how to drill correctly, and was even named first corporal of cadets, the class leader, at the end of the year. However, he was still a poor student.

Marshall's strengths were practical, not academic. Once, when the cadets were given the day off in com-memoration of the Civil War battle of New Market, Marshall lobbied his friends into following him on a little adventure into the countryside that surrounded their fortress-like school in Lexington, Virginia. He wouldn't tell his comrades where they were going or what they were doing. His friends assumed that they were in for a fun day of hiking or fishing.

Marshall's idea of a good time differed significantly from that of the normal student; his big surprise was giving his friends a lesson about the battle that had won them the day off. Standing on the spot where the fight had taken place only a few decades earlier, Marshall outlined where the opposing forces had been positioned and how the battle developed. Pointing over the land-scape, he indicated the geographic features that played a key part in the conflict. His friends were disappointed. Though VMI was a military university akin to West Point, most of its graduates went on to civilian rather than military careers. Most didn't get excited about military theory. Marshall, on the other hand, was enthused. He had found his calling.

Through the rest of his years at VMI, Marshall did well enough in history and geography (though he still only ranked in the middle of his class of forty-seven), but he was better known as a leader. Each year, he was elected the com

Marshall in 1900, while a student at VMI. *(Courtesy of the George C. Marshall Foundation.)*

manding student of his class, getting promoted from first corporal to first sergeant and finally to first captain of the cadet corps, the most important, highest-ranking student at the school.

Marshall was beginning to internalize the characteristics of being a good military leader. Even in college he recognized how being friends with someone might ultimately make it more difficult to command them. Consequently, many fellow students remembered him the way others did in the years to come: distant, aloof, and mostly alone.

Later he would say, "What I learned at VMI was self-control, discipline, so that it was ground in. I learned also the problem of managing men."

Marshall's leadership did not go untested. Following a tactic that had recently been used at West Point, the VMI students suddenly fell silent one night at dinner. This unnerving quiet was a sign of disrespect that challenged Marshall to take control and restore a sense of normalcy to the situation. Just as he had pulled the plug on the raft years before, Marshall promptly ordered the students to attention and marched them out of the mess hall. At the time, they had been enjoying a special treat of strawberries. Their impudence cost them their dessert and taught them a lesson: George Marshall was a quick-thinking leader. He later commented that the cadets "would judge you severely if you proved to be a slack performer in the business of your military duties."

Of all the people who surrounded young George Marshall Jr. at VMI, the person with whom he grew closest during his time in Lexington did not live within the school's confines. One day, while walking around town, Marshall heard someone playing a piano. He stopped to listen outside the house and was so entranced by the music that he made a habit of returning. Finally, the door was opened and he was welcomed inside to make the acquaintance of the pianist, the beautiful Elizabeth "Lily" Carter Coles.

The daughter of a well-known family, the fair-skinned twenty-six-year-old Lily was usually kept at home growing up. She suffered from a serious heart condition that constantly threatened her life. Despite her poor health, many men, including George's older brother, Stuart, had vied for her attention. However, it was the tall, quiet cadet with the captain's insignia that she was taken with, reputedly saying after she first met George Marshall, "I intend to marry him." The feeling was mutual, and George would often sneak out of VMI to see her. As this was against the rules, he risked expulsion for his clandestine visits. Asked later why he took such a risk, he replied simply, "I was much in love."

George intended to propose to Lily. He knew that he needed to get a job if he was going to support a family. The only problem was that Marshall had his heart set on a military career, and there were few commissions to be had in the small peacetime army. His only option was to land one of the few slots.

TWO

BRILLIANT YOUNG OFFICER

At the conclusion of the Spanish-American War in 1898, the United States found itself in possession of several foreign territories, including the Philippines in the eastern Pacific. Although the victory ushered in a new era of American military might, the United States planned to decrease the size of its military after the war. However, while troops were no longer needed to fight the Spanish, it turned out that they were still needed to stabilize the newly won territories.

The Filipinos had been very unhappy under the Spanish and soon rose in active resistance against the Americans. In response, the U.S. increased the size of the army from 65,000 in 1899 to 100,000 by 1901. This meant the army needed 837 new first and second lieutenants.

Upon graduating in 1901, Marshall wanted one of the

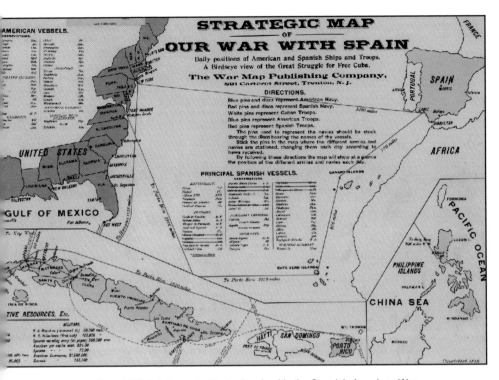

This map from 1898 details the territories involved in the Spanish-American War, including Cuba and the Philippines. *(Library of Congress)*

commissions. Getting a job as a junior officer would be the first step in a military career. It would also give him the financial stability to marry Lily. Although he was an exemplary cadet leader at a military institution, Marshall was not guaranteed one of the prized officer jobs. These new commissions would go to West Point graduates first, then to candidates already in the army, then to former officers and volunteers, and then, last of all, to Marshall's category: qualified civilians. All applicants save for West Point graduates had to pass an exam to be considered.

The problem that Marshall faced was that taking the exam required a letter of authorization—effectively an invitation—from the War Department. Simply getting the letter required political connections.

Marshall's parents were opposed to his decision to join the army. His father only relented when he was convinced that his son would make a fine soldier. Inquiring as to his son's qualifications, George Sr. received a letter from VMI's superintendent, General Shipp, that said, "If commissioned in the Army, young Marshall will, in all respects, soon take his stand much above the average West Point graduate."

Reassured of his son's choice, George Sr. took it upon himself to use his network of political contacts to get his son one of the few examination slots. Having assembled letters of recommendation and introduction, George Jr. made the trip to Washington, D.C., the April before his graduation in order to further his cause with the decision makers. He met with Philander C. Knox, the attorney general and a friend of his father. Then, demonstrating courage and self-assurance—not to mention a desire to cut through red tape—he barged in on a reception to try to speak with John A. Hull, the chairman of the House Military Affairs Committee. He did manage to see Hull but felt that little came from their impromptu meeting. Undaunted, he marched into the White House on a mission to see President William McKinley.

Marshall remembered his visit this way: "I had no appointment of any kind . . . The old colored man [the head usher] asked me if I had an appointment and I told him I didn't. He said I would never get in, that there wasn't any possibil- ity. I sat there and watched people, some ten or fifteen, go in by appointment, stay ten minutes, and be excused. Finally a man and his daughter went in . . . I attached myself to the tail of the pro- cession and gained the President's of- fice. The old col- ored man frowned at me on his way

President William McKinley.

out but I stood pat. After the people had met the President they also went out, leaving me standing there. Mr. McKinley in a very nice manner asked what I wanted and I stated my case. I don't recall what he said, but from that I think flowed my appointment or rather my author- ity to appear for examination."

Marshall never knew if McKinley did anything to help out the impetuous cadet who had snuck into his office, but just before graduation in June 1901, Marshall's name appeared on the list of civilians invited to take the test. Soon thereafter, Marshall took the exam and passed—though again his deficiencies in formal educa- tion were evident. In January 1902, Marshall's commission as a second lieutenant was confirmed. Plans were made for a quick wedding, and George and Lily were married on February 11. They took the train to Washington, D.C., for what they believed would be a one-day honeymoon, because George had to report for duty on February 13. Luckily, the army extended his honeymoon to ten days—a change that was welcomed by the newlyweds, as George was about to be sent to the Philippines for two years while Lily would return home to her family in Lexington.

George and Lily's wedding day on February 11, 1902. *From left to right:* Marie, Lily, George Jr., Stuart, Laura, George Sr., and Elizabeth Coles, Lily's mother. *(Courtesy of the George C. Marshall Foundation.)*

When their honeymoon was over, Lily and George said their good-byes. After journeying across the country, Marshall set sail from San Francisco on April 12, 1902, to join the Thirtieth Infantry Regiment, Company G, in the Philippines. He was to take command of fifty men on the island of Mindoro. Perhaps the most harrowing part of his posting was simply getting there. Sailing on a steamer through a typhoon, Marshall and another

This map of the Philippines from the early 1900s shows the island of Mindoro, where Marshall was stationed from 1902 to 1903. *(Library of Congress)*

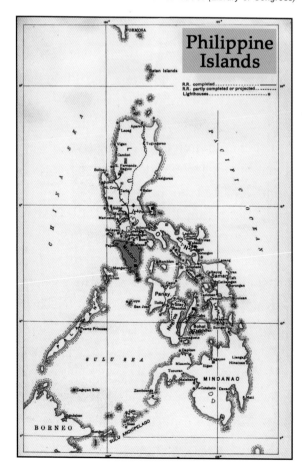

American soldier had to take command of the ship after the Filipino who was steering broke his ribs, leaving the boat without a captain. Of the storm, Marshall said, "I am not exaggerating when I say that the boat would tilt over until the longboats on the upper deck would go into the water. It would just poise there for a little bit as if it would never go back again. Then it would roll to the other side."

Mindoro was much calmer. The islands were now mostly at peace, save for a few insurgent fighters and armed robbers. Commanders like Marshall were largely fighting boredom and apathy among their troops. It was a good opportunity to showcase his faculty for organization and planning. At the time, the Philippines were beset by an epidemic of cholera, a potentially fatal intestinal disease. The best way to fight cholera was to maintain a clean living environment, which Marshall resolved that his unit would do. His persistence paid off, and the unit suffered no fatalities.

The epidemic meant the men had to be quarantined, which made them restless. Morale was low. To break the monotony, Marshall planned a Fourth of July celebration. At first the troops did not want to participate, but when Marshall started awarding generous cash prizes, collected from the officers, the soldiers clamored to participate in the day's games and events, making the celebration a minor success.

After moving among several other postings in the Philippines, Marshall returned stateside in November

1903. He was assigned first to Fort Reno in Oklahoma and then to Fort Clark, Texas. He and Lily were reunited, but supporting a family was not easy. At the time, a second lieutenant made $116.67 a month, not bad for the day. But from this amount, he had to buy almost everything he needed, including his own military equipment.

The assignment at Fort Clark—making detailed maps of the hot desolate landscape of southwestern Texas— was hard and boring. The desert temperatures went well past one hundred degrees Fahrenheit. In fact, it was so hot that Marshall lost more than thirty pounds off his 170-pound frame. He called the assignment "the hardest service I ever had in the army." Marshall distinguished himself by making some of the best maps that had come out of the project. His superior called his map "the best one received and the only complete one." Years later this assignment would prove beneficial as Marshall devised strategy for battles around the world, carefully developing an appreciation for the importance of terrain. The assignment also taught him about red tape in the military—simply getting provisions for a trip into the desert was a process that wandered through various jurisdictions and could take weeks.

With assignments in the Philippines and the Southwest under his belt, Marshall, now twenty-five years old, had proven to be a capable young officer and was invited to attend the School of the Line at Fort Leavenworth, Kansas, in August 1906. A recommendation to Leavenworth was a sign that Second Lieutenant Marshall was on a fast track in the army. The School of the Line was a one-year program designed to give an excellent general military education to those able to withstand its rigors. The program was intensely competitive, and Marshall was lucky to get in. Soon after he was admitted, the rules were changed to require that new students hold at least the rank of captain, a rank that Marshall would not obtain for another ten years.

In Marshall's long career in the army, this was one of the few examples where it seemed that good luck was on his side. His rise through the ranks was usually the result of putting in his time rather than catching lucky breaks. Until World War II, advancing through the ranks was not the result of how smart one was or how well one could lead others but of how long an officer had been in the army. It took great leaders and terrible leaders the same amount of time to be promoted. There were many senior officers who were given significant responsibilities based solely on their years in uniform rather than their abilities. For the gifted Marshall, this system would prove to be a major source of frustration throughout his career.

At the prestigious School of the Line, Marshall would learn how to be a better officer. He would learn how to command more effectively and study military tactics and strategy. Marshall also benefited from getting to know other officers that had been handpicked for the school; they were a select group that were older, more experienced, and able to offer advice and guidance to a younger soldier. In the relatively small world of the early-1900s army, Marshall would often run across former classmates and instructors from Leavenworth.

Soon after arriving in Kansas, Marshall overheard two classmates discussing who would perform the best at Leavenworth. He was surprised to find his own name ignored. Just as he had previously vowed to do the family name proud at VMI, Marshall set a goal to out-perform the rest of his classmates at the School of the Line. In his quest, he was partly aided by the inspiration that he drew from Major John F. Morrison. An unconventional teacher with new and exciting ideas, Morrison was respected for his practical instruction. Later, those who had learned under him would proudly refer to themselves as "Morrison Men."

As much as Marshall enjoyed the atmosphere at the school and the teachings of Morrison, making good on his goal was a challenge. Speaking of his time at Leavenworth, Marshall said, "I finally got into the habit of study, which I never really had before. I revived what little I had carried with me out of college and I became pretty automatic at the business . . . [but] it was the hardest work I ever did in my life." Although he was one of the youngest and least experienced, Marshall graduated first in his class—a dramatic improvement from VMI only a few years before, where he was a lackluster, middle-of-the-pack student. Marshall had found something that was important to him.

As a result of his stellar performance at the School

A bird's-eye view of the city of Leavenworth, Kansas, looking across the Missouri River. *(Library of Congress)*

of the Line, Marshall was invited to the more advanced second year of schooling for the best students: Staff College at Leavenworth. During this year, from 1907-1908, Marshall again so impressed the staff that he was invited back to instruct at the school. Even though he was promoted to the rank of first lieutenant in 1907, he was still outranked by almost every other student and instructor at the school.

Marshall would remain at Leavenworth until 1910, instructing during the school year and helping to train National Guard units during the summers. The modern equivalent of the state militias from the country's colonial days, the National Guard was tasked with creating a citizen-soldier force that could be deployed locally to protect life and property. Like his mentor, Major

Morrison, Marshall was acclaimed as a good teacher who stressed practical methods and made his students think. Many of the men who studied under the young Lieutenant Marshall would later go on to form the top echelon of leadership in the army. Arriving at new posts, Marshall would often find that his superior officers were also his former students.

At the conclusion of his time at Leavenworth, Marshall took a notable assignment with the Massachusetts Volunteer Militia where he was involved with planning National Guard maneuvers. Not only did this assignment expose him to training nonprofessional soldiers, it also gave him the opportunity to participate in much bigger practice battles with the regular forces than he otherwise would have, given his lowly rank.

Being in the army meant a regular rotation of posts, so after a summer in Massachusetts, Marshall was on his way again. In August 1913, he was sent back to the Philippines, this time with the Thirteenth Infantry Division.

Surrounded by the monotony of garrison life and uninterested in the limited social offerings available to him, Marshall spent some of his free time analyzing Filipino battlefields, old maps, and reports in order to get a better understanding of how to fight. It was study that would come in handy again and again during his career. Marshall was also a good student of the military in general, as he proved in several instances.

Marshall once wagered another soldier that, during drill, the inspecting officer would find three relatively minor, cosmetic faults with his unit—one soldier who was unshaven, one whose shirt was unbuttoned, and one without a bayonet. Marshall also bet his colleague that the officer would fail to note three serious tactical errors that Marshall would make on purpose during his field exercises. Just as Marshall predicted, the minor faults were harped upon while the major issues that may have cost lives went unnoticed. This underscored how amateurish the army was and helped cement Marshall's reputation for insight. Though this incident greatly impressed his peers, in later years Marshall regretted that his actions had made the inspecting officer look foolish.

The second incident that brought Marshall fame in the Philippines took place during practice maneuvers in January 1914. Large mock battles are regularly planned in order to give soldiers and their commanding officers a taste of what a battle might be like—albeit without real bullets. Marshall was assigned as an assistant to the "white force," which was tasked with a proposed invasion of Luzon. As fate would have it, when the big day of the maneuvers arrived, Marshall's commander became sick and someone was needed to take over his responsibilities. The job of commanding nearly 5,000 men fell to the young George Marshall.

At the time, Lieutenant Marshall wrote home, "I had an opportunity that rarely ever comes to a Colonel."

Taking the reins of leadership, Marshall amazed his colleagues with a display of command that was so in-

Marshall worked with Henry "Hap" Arnold throughout his career.

sightful, methodical, and well executed that it seemed as if he had been leading the exercise the whole time. Although the forces under his command managed little more than a draw versus the defending army, Marshall's reputation had been established. He was discovered to be a gifted planner and a capable leader—an officer others thought of as someone they would want on their side.

Observing the demonstration was Lieutenant Henry H. "Hap" Arnold, later chief of the Army Air Forces in World War II. Writing home to his wife about the maneuvers, Arnold declared that he had seen a future chief of staff at work.

Though the Philippines exercise was just a war game, Marshall wound up in the hospital afterward. Stressed-out and overworked, he spent two weeks in bed recovering from his exhaustion. This was followed by two months of sick leave as well as an additional two months' regular leave. Taking advantage of the time off, George and Lily took a vacation in the Far East. The tour brought them to Japan, Manchuria, and Korea—all of which would play a much bigger role in his life than he could have imagined in 1914.

Mixing business with pleasure while in Japan, Marshall took the opportunity to study battlefields from the Russo-Japanese War (1904-1905). At Leavenworth, Marshall had become interested in that conflict, an interest he shared with Major Morrison. The war had started with a Japanese surprise attack on the Russian naval fleet.

While Marshall was visiting, relations between the United States and Japan were strained. Even so, Marshall found the Japanese soldiers helpful and friendly, re-marking, "Japanese officers . . . treated me royally." He came away with a new respect for the Japanese, particu-larly their training methods, and felt that the American army could learn from their techniques.

Just as a star athlete might put in more time alone after practice has ended, incidents like this highlight Marshall's thirst for knowledge and his desire to be a better soldier. This pattern of never leaving his profes-sional life at the office was to surface again and again. Once, while vacationing with Lily's parents, Marshall devoted himself to making a detailed terrain map of the vacation property.

Back in the Philippines, Marshall was transferred to Brigadier General Hunter Liggett's command. They had known each other at Leavenworth. As he continued to prove himself extremely capable, Marshall was steadily gaining a cadre of supporters within the army.

Even though Marshall was promoted to captain in October 1916—only his second promotion since joining the army in 1902—and was admired by all those around him, he was thirty-five and continuously frustrated by the lack of progress in his career. In October 1915, he had written to a friend: "The absolute stagnation in promotion in the infantry has caused me to make tentative plans for resigning . . . the prospects for advancement in the Army are so restricted by law and by the accumulation of large numbers of men of nearly the same age all in a single grade, that I do not feel it right to waste all my best years in the vain struggle against insurmountable difficulties."

One of the recurring themes of Marshall's career was that while he won near-universal acclaim for his exceptional abilities to command and manage, this acclaim did not translate into faster promotions. Over the course of his career, many of his colleagues would lobby for his promotion but without success because of the army's antiquated promotion system.

Outside of seniority, the surest way to win promotion was to serve with distinction in battle. Few soldiers relish the idea of going to war, but for Marshall and others in his position, looming world events indicated that they might soon be forced to put their years of training to the test.

THREE

PREPARATIONS

The conditions that eventually erupted into World War I had been developing in Europe for decades. Two old, cumbersome empires—the Austro-Hungarian in Central Europe and the Ottoman in Eastern Europe and the Middle East—were coming apart. New powerful nation-states emerging from the industrialization of the nineteenth century were clashing over possession of faraway colonies in Asia and Africa. Germany, recently united around the mighty Prussian military, was anxious to flex its muscle and expand its sphere of influence in Europe. Russia, with its antiquated political system and slowly developing economy, was still determined to spread its influence into the Balkan states at the expense of Austria and Turkey. France was still seething from the humiliation it received from Germany in the Franco-

Prussian War of 1870-1871. The smaller states in Europe, such as Belgium, signed treaties with Great Britain and other nations that promised to protect them in case of attack from Germany or Russia.

By the summer of 1914, Europe was a powder keg with a long fuse snaking into the most volatile region on the continent, the tiny Balkan states. On the morning of June 28, 1914, in Sarajevo, the capital city of Bosnia, which had recently been annexed by Austria, the Archduke Francis Ferdinand, heir to the Austro-Hungarian

Europe in 1911, three years before the outbreak of World War I. *(Library of Congress)*

The beautiful Eastern European city of Sarajevo, where Archduke Ferdinand and his wife were assassinated on June 28, 1914. *(Library of Congress)*

throne, was visiting to inspect the troops. As a car was taking the archduke and his wife, Sophie, to the town hall, a Serbian nationalist named Gavrilo Princip pulled a pistol and assassinated Ferdinand and his wife.

Although there was no evidence of collaboration by Serbian officials in the actions of Gavrilo Princip, who was not a government agent, the Austrian government, pressured by the Germans, declared war on Serbia on July 28. Russia, which had agreed to fight on Serbia's side, began to mobilize; Germany, allied with Austria, declared war on Russia on August 1. Soon France and Great Britain, who were also ensnared in the alliance system that had developed over the previous generation, were drawn into the conflict. World War I had begun.

After a few weeks of rapid attacks by the Germans and Austrians to the west and the east, the war ground to a bloody, terrible stalemate. By Christmas 1914, the western front had stabilized into a line of trenches stretching from the English Channel to Switzerland. This is where the war in the west stayed for three years. In the east, the ill-prepared Russian army suffered a series of defeats, but the Germans and Austrians were not able to deliver a knockout punch.

The European conflict made headlines across the Atlantic, but few Americans had any interest in joining the fray. The more pressing concern was across the Rio Grande.

In 1910, Porfirio Diaz was reelected president of Mexico—a post he had held or controlled since 1876. Over the course of the next year, Diaz's political rival, Francisco Madero, organized a revolution that removed Diaz from power in May 1911 after six months of fighting. Much of Madero's success was the result of the support of regional and military leaders, whom he either ignored or feuded with once he was in power. As a result, the next two years saw six revolts until Madero was overthrown, followed by four years of counterrevolutions, political instability, and shifting allegiances between a half-dozen potential leaders. Mexico was embroiled in constant civil war.

Among those vying for power was Pancho Villa. After the United States threw its support to a rival faction, Villa became incensed. He was determined to take revenge.

Mexican revolutionary Pancho Villa.

On January 9, 1916, a band of Villa's men stopped a train carrying American mine employees in Mexico and murdered fifteen of them. Exactly two months later, a band of nearly five hundred of Villa's men was sent to attack the town of Columbus, New Mexico, killing eighteen Americans.

This last action spurred President Woodrow Wilson to assign General John J. "Black Jack" Pershing to lead a so-called punitive expedition of more than 6,000 men to subdue Villa. Advancing hundreds of miles into Mexico, American forces were finally confronted by Mexican troops and orders came to withdraw in January of 1917.

When Marshall returned to the states in May 1916, tensions were running high in the United States as a result of news stories from Mexico and Europe. Although the Mexican situation was being contained, that was not the case in Europe. Despite being protected by the wide expanse of the Atlantic Ocean, the fear among isolationist-minded Americans was that the United States would be engulfed in the European war.

Many Americans did not want to see this happen. President Wilson was reelected in 1916 on the slogan "He kept us out of war." But even before the election, German U-boats (submarines) sank the passenger ship *Lusitania* on May 7, 1915. Of the 1,198 people killed, 128 were American citizens. Germany promised to continue targeting passenger ships suspected of taking supplies to Great Britain.

As war became likely, it was clear that America needed to bulk up its military. Untested, the military was unpre-

The German attack on the *Lusitania* was widely used to muster popular support for American involvement in the conflict in Europe. *(Library of Congress)*

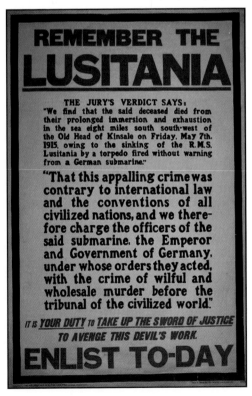

pared for combat. One of the biggest problems was a lack of soldiers and trained officers to lead them. Marshall found himself assigned to Major General J. Franklin Bell. He was to help set up training camps for soldiers-to-be, first in Monterey, California, and then in Salt Lake City, Utah.

As had been his style while teaching at Leavenworth, Marshall believed in thorough, pragmatic, and practical lessons. Marshall worried that students would look for a single answer and fail to act in a timely manner. Textbooks could never predict what a commander might actually encounter in battle.

The Monterey training facility was located at the Del Monte Hotel, a luxurious locale with a beautiful ocean view. Marshall inherited a group of volunteer recruits that had been inspired to do their part to help out their

The opulent Del Monte Hotel in Monterey.

country. They had even paid their own way to the training center. These were affluent young men who felt the pull of patriotism—and the allure and adventure of playing soldier. General Bell noted, "I saw more Rolls-Royces and other fine cars around there than I have ever seen collected."

As they were there of their own free will and had paid for this adventure, it was difficult to justify working the recruits hard or making them uncomfortable and risk alienating them. Marshall solved the problem by setting an example of a real military lifestyle. Arriving at the hotel, he forewent the plush accommodations in favor of setting up a tent in the yard. The idea soon caught on among the recruits.

He would not settle for having them "play" soldier. Addressing the volunteers at dinner, he said, "You fellows came down here because you were enthusiastic to do something in this time of emergency, and you are paying your own expenses. This morning you were in a maneuver and you hardly marched at all. You were in reserve, sitting around resting. Then your wives and girls all brought out good things and you had champagne, and it has been quite delightful to sit under the trees. Now you are so exhausted by this war service that you can't do a damn thing. I'm going to go out there and drill you again, and if you can't drill, I am going to march you in and report you as wholly ineffective."

Marshall worked the men hard but discovered that they enjoyed it. The volunteers even began calling their leader "Dynamite." Marshall next took on a similar training role at Fort Douglas in Utah under Lieutenant Colonel Johnson Hagood. After Monterey, Marshall now had a better understanding of the process of turning civilians into soldiers.

The brief training camp in Utah showed Hagood his subordinate's singular talents. Responding to the question of whether he would wish to have Marshall serve under him, Hagood wrote, "Yes, but I would prefer to serve *under his command."* He went on to recommend that Marshall be made "a brigadier [one-star] general in the regular Army," adding, "Every day this is postponed is a loss to the Army and the nation."

Hagood was blunt: "The army and the nation sorely needs such men in the grade of general Officer at this time, and if I had the power I would nominate him to fill the next vacancy in the grade of Brigadier General." Though Hagood and others petitioned on Marshall's behalf, there were nearly two thousand men ahead of him in the standard promotion order.

In Monterey and Salt Lake City, Marshall added another strength to his resume: he became a talented trainer and administrator. In his role as instructor to new recruits, Marshall saw how unprepared the army was and came to understand how difficult it was to raise an army from scratch. He sharpened his ability to bring new recruits up to fighting form quickly.

In early 1917, all of the training seemed a prudent measure, given that the Germans had continued their policy of unrestricted submarine warfare, targeting all ships regardless of nationality or cargo. President Wilson could delay no longer. He asked Congress for a declaration of war, saying the world must be made safe for democracy. War was officially declared on April 6, 1917.

Marshall and others had, up to this point, been training what volunteers and adventure seekers they could. Yet their numbers were not large enough to field an adequate and formidable army. In June of 1917, the United States conducted a draft. The country's young men were required to register for a lottery in which they would be assigned a number. If their number was called, they had to join the military. Of the many millions who registered for the draft, only 2.8 million were actually selected, about half a million of whom were inducted in 1917.

The draft was necessary because

A 1917 recruitment poster for the American Armed Forces. *(Library of Congress)*

not enough men wanted to join the military. Pressing them into service—and putting them in harm's way—to fight a conflict that isolationist Americans saw as Europe's problem did not make for an enthusiastic corps.

Marshall was of a different mind. War was what he had been training for and it presented some real opportunities for him. Though averse to pulling strings, he wanted desperately to go to France and gain some real battle experience. With the help of influential friends in the army—many of whom he met at Leavenworth—his wish was granted and he was assigned to the staff of the First Division. The First was, appropriately, the first division of a few thousand men sent to Europe; by the end of the war, the total American force there would number forty-two divisions. After his commanding officer, Marshall was the second American from the First Division to land on French soil as the first wave of troops arrived at the end of June.

On the boat it soon became clear just how unprepared the United States was for this war. As men were being shipped to France, makeshift combat units were still being assembled on board. While it seemed to Marshall that the navy (on whose boat he was being transported) was well organized, he overheard a sailor say that they carried no ammunition for the boat's guns. For Marshall, this was a disturbing revelation.

FOUR

WORLD WAR I

Despite the warm welcome that the troops received from the besieged French people, the first U.S. detachment was little more than window dressing. These troops, many of whom had not been properly trained and were assigned to their new units on the day they disembarked, were not ready for battle. They still needed months of training before they could relieve the exhausted French soldiers who had been fighting the Germans for over two years. It would be more than a year after Congress declared war before an American division moved into combat.

Rather than prepare the troops at home, the army thought it was best to send them to France and train them behind the front lines. This would give the troops the chance to train near real battlefields and would also help buoy Allied morale. The training centers could also draw on the expertise of the more experienced French troops. A U.S. Army memo stated:

> If the French army is to be our model and if the American is to fight beside the Frenchman according to the latter's methods, then the training of the American troops should be done in as close contact as possible with the French troops, not only from the technical point of view but from that of mutual acquaintance, mutual understanding, and mutual respect . . . The French divisions, while in these camps, are constantly in training and bring with them the latest methods from the front. Our officers and men can see each day the practical work of the French, can talk freely with their French comrades, can get French experts to come over, assist and advise and in general live in the midst of the French veteran troops while these latter are training.

Having demonstrated his ability to train raw recruits during assignments with National Guard units and volunteer training camps, Marshall, working under General William Sibert, was again given the task of turning new soldiers into a formidable fighting force. Getting the new men trained was challenging. Even though both the Americans and the Allied nations wanted to get the Americans into battle as soon as possible, the army lacked proper supplies.

On one occasion in October 1917, General Pershing, the commanding American general in France, exploded

General John J. "Black Jack" Pershing. *(Library of Congress)*

out of frustration at what he perceived as incompetence and unpreparedness on the part of General Sibert. Marshall saw the dressing down of his commander as unfair. As he began to explain this calmly to Pershing, the legendary general turned away, ignoring the younger man.

Pershing was a veteran of the Spanish-American War, had just spent nearly a year commanding troops in Mexico, and was the ranking army officer in France. Even so, Marshall, displaying some of the pluck and gumption of his youth, was not about to let Pershing walk away. Grabbing the high-ranking U.S. officer by the arm, Marshall insisted, "General Pershing, there's something to be said here and I think I should say it because I've been here longest." What came next happened so fast that Marshall didn't remember exactly what he said to Pershing. Similarly, the other soldiers who were there remembered not so much what Marshall said but rather that he would dare say anything—particularly in such an aggressive manner—to Pershing. They did remember that his speech was fast and peppered with facts, a style that many would associate with him in his later years.

When Marshall finished his tirade, Pershing remarked, "You must appreciate the troubles we have."

To this, Marshall impetuously shot back, "Yes, General, but we have them every day and they have to be solved before night." They were doing the best they could with few resources and little time, Marshall said.

Marshall's fellow officers believed that this behavior would surely end their colleague's career. Marshall knew it was likely to put him out of favor. But Marshall's honest confrontation impressed Pershing, who valued a soldier unafraid to speak the truth. On future visits, Pershing would seek out Marshall. He knew he could trust the young officer. Marshall was ultimately transferred to Pershing's headquarters, where he was to benefit from the tutelage and mentorship of one of the country's military leaders. Like Pershing, Marshall was serious and focused and had a desire to get things done. His career would eventually mirror Pershing's—aided by the latter's advice—and their close relationship would continue until Black Jack's death in 1948.

After months of training, the Americans were ready to rotate some of their troops onto the front lines to relieve the French. For three years, the French had withstood the rigors of living and fighting in trenches. World War I was a new kind of war, marked by its grand scale, global involvement, and use of new technologies, including motor vehicles and poison gas. Some nine million soldiers—nearly one in every eight mobilized—would be killed during the conflict, averaging more than 5,000 deaths per day. Many who did not suffer fatal wounds were terribly scarred. The British alone saw 240,000 soldiers crippled by leg or arm amputations.

In early November, the first American troops were sent to a relatively quiet part of the front. Only twelve days later, the Germans mounted a surprise attack, killing three Americans and capturing a dozen more. Marshall made the trip to the battlefield in order to study what had happened; the dead Americans had not even been removed when he arrived.

Marshall was promoted to the rank of major in November 1917 and got the silver leaves of a lieutenant colonel just after Christmas. He was subsequently promoted to full colonel on September 21, 1918. This was a very rapid increase in rank, and many believed it well deserved. There was, however, a downside.

During wartime, the military grew larger. A larger army required more officers at all levels. Aside from simply needing more men in command, more promotions were granted as officers were killed in battle. But knowing that the military could not afford to keep so large a force and so many senior officers during peacetime, a special wartime promotion system was developed. Soldiers were granted temporary promotions; after the conflict was over, an officer would return to his original, pre-conflict rank. For Marshall this meant that he would return to being a lowly captain at the war's end. In addition to the frustration of losing his rank after the war, Marshall found it particularly irksome that his repeated requests for combat command were rebuffed. Prestige and permanent promotions were won by commanders on the front lines, not those who did paperwork and planning far from the battlefield.

When he was assigned to the First Division, Marshall's job required him to keep headquarters informed about activity on the front as well as supplies and morale. He would walk the muddy front lines in his heavy raincoat, carrying a revolver, some food rations, and the all-important gas mask. But after each expedition, he would return to his desk. His senior commanding officers knew Marshall was capable of battlefield command, but they believed that he had a special talent for staff work and was more valuable performing those functions. At one point, General Bullard wrote with regard to staff work, "I doubt that in this, whether it be teaching or practice,

[Marshall] has an equal in the Army today." Marshall was a victim of his own abilities.

In contrast, while Marshall was sitting in headquarters hoping for a field command, another young officer, Douglas MacArthur, was making a name for himself in the muddy trenches. MacArthur was the son of Arthur MacArthur, the legendary Civil War hero who had served as commander of the Philippines following the Spanish-American War. But Douglas MacArthur was not going to rely on his good name to win promotions. He relished combat. He even went "over the top" of the trenches into combat with his men, unarmed. His biographer explained: "He could hardly be said to have dressed for the occasion. He wore his smashed-down cap instead of a steel helmet, and the rest of his outfit was outlandish by standards of the western front: a four-foot muffler knitted by his mother, a turtleneck sweater, immaculate riding breeches, and cavalry boots with a mirror finish. From his mouth a cigarette holder jutted at a jaunty angle. His only weapon was a riding crop." MacArthur was an old-fashioned military leader who relished his role as warrior.

For Marshall, the fact that he not been sent to the front and instead branded a staff officer was not only unfortunate but also ironic. From his days at VMI, he had shown the makings of an exceptional leader of men.

After catching Pershing's eye, Marshall was transferred to General Headquarters in July 1918. There, while serving under Colonel Fox Conner, Operations

Section chief, and Colonel Hugh A. Drum, chief of staff of the First Army, he was responsible for planning a series of major offensives that were stunning in their logistic and strategic complexity.

Marshall's job was to coordinate American troop movements with the French and the British. During 1917, Russia was wracked with two revolutions. The final one led to a seizure of power by the Communists, who immediately agreed to a unilateral peace with the Germans. This could have been devastating to the Allies, because it freed the Germans from having to fight in the east. It was critical that the British, French, and Americans organize for the concentrated German attack as well as prepare for the massive offensive that would be necessary to end the war victoriously.

It was a stressful time. Allied forces had to win two major battles at nearly the same time. The Americans had to defeat the Germans at Saint-Mihiel. This would be the first major action under American command, and victory was crucial for morale. The French planned an

Ruins in Saint-Mihiel, France, where Marshall stopped the advance of German troops. *(Library of Congress)*

offensive at Meuse-Argonne that, if successful, would begin pushing the Germans back eastward and allow them to capture iron deposits and retake important rail lines.

After stopping the German advance at Saint-Mihiel (at a cost of 13,000 dead and wounded), Marshall and the planners needed to move 600,000 men to the next battle in less than ten days. More than 400,000 troops rushed from the Saint-Mihiel area to Meuse-Argonne. The transfer required exact planning and vast resources. In addition to the motorized vehicles, the shift required 90,000 animals to carry equipment. To complicate matters, Marshall could only move the force at night so as to avoid detection. Marshall dove into the monumental task and soon earned the nickname "wizard."

The war was coming to a rapid end, however. The Germans had bet everything on one final offensive in the west. They had hoped that the troops they brought in from the east would be enough to win before the full strength of the Americans could be organized. But the failure to capitalize on the Russian surrender at the battles at Saint-Mihiel and Meuse-Argonne revealed that the German army was exhausted. The German commander, General Erich Ludendorff, near a nervous breakdown, resigned at the end of October 1918, and Austria and Turkey admitted defeat in the following weeks. Finally, without a decisive final battle having been fought, at 11 AM on November, 11, 1918, the victorious Allied armies reached an armistice with Germany. The

This painting by Herbert Olivier depicts the signing of the Treaty of Versailles on June 28, 1919. *(Versailles, France)*

fighting was over, but the official end of the war would not come until June 1919 when the Treaty of Versailles was signed.

The end of the war signaled a new chapter in both U.S. and European affairs. France was devastated, and other nations had paid dearly as well. An entire generation of men had been lost. To pay for the great conflict, the combatant governments had gone into great debt. At Versailles, Germany was forced to accept responsibility for the war and agreed to pay burdensome reparations— payments to its former enemies to cover the cost of the war—although Germany had lost much of its manpower and industry, and faced its own war debt.

Unscathed on its own soil and a late entrant to the conflict (though it did lose more than 100,000 men), the United States emerged as a major world power. While the rest of the world's most powerful countries had been nearly ruined, the U.S. had become a major commercial force, both in terms of the production of goods and the granting of credit. The United States was faced with the responsibility of being the world's dominant country. Hoping to share some of this burden of leadership, President Wilson pushed for the adoption of the League of Nations as a global forum to resolve issues and prevent the sort of conflict that had just ended.

The war had also redrawn the map. Germany lost colonies, and the Austro-Hungarian and Ottoman Empires were carved into several smaller, independent countries in Central and Eastern Europe and the Middle East.

For Marshall, the war did not change his fortunes as he had hoped. Before sailing for France in 1917, it looked as if participating in the conflict would speed up his frustratingly slow rise through the ranks. But not having a battlefield command hurt him. He saw contemporaries who had the responsibilities of commanding men in battle—such as Douglas MacArthur—elevated to the permanent rank of general. Marshall, on the other hand, was reduced to his prewar rank of captain after the war (though he was soon re-promoted to major).

The Treaty of Versailles redefined many European borders.

There were more intangible benefits, however. Though Marshall missed out on rapid promotion, his wartime experience would eventually prove to be far more valuable than a general's star. He had seen firsthand how difficult it was to create and train an army. He had struggled with the tactical, strategic, and logistic issues faced by an army once it was in the field. Most importantly, he had learned how to solve seemingly intractable challenges.

At war's end, Marshall joined in the celebrations that spread across Europe and the United States. As a member of Pershing's headquarters staff, he participated in parades, met foreign leaders and dignitaries—including Winston Churchill in London—went on speaking tours, and received various commendations, including the French Legion of Honor. However, with the end of hostilities, Marshall also saw his career fall into a lull.

Pershing asked Marshall to serve as his aide. For the next five years, Marshall was to be at Pershing's side in Washington, D.C., while Black Jack served as the U.S. Army chief of staff, the president's senior army advisor and, effectively, the head of the army.

Though his troops had been victorious in war, Pershing knew that reforms were needed. Looking back on the war, it was clear that a small American army, supplemented by draftees, was not a feasible plan. It had taken a full year to train the new soldiers. Pershing pushed for universal military training (UMT), an idea that Marshall also embraced and would continue to support for the rest of his life. The premise of UMT was simple: require men to join the military at eighteen and be properly trained, and then discharge them after a limited amount of time with the option to recall these trained troops should the need arise.

To Marshall's way of thinking, this was a workable solution to two very thorny issues. First, UMT would facilitate a faster military buildup in a time of war because new recruits would not need to be trained from square one. Second, it would resolve the American cultural and societal problem of maintaining a large standing army. Military service would be required of all men, cutting across economic and cultural lines.

While a large standing army—a force maintained in both war and peace—would drastically reduce the time between when troops were needed and when they could actually be deployed, the concept presented two major issues. The first was cost; an army of one million men would be very expensive. Second, a large standing army was seen as being incompatible with a true democracy because the military could potentially be turned against the country by nefarious commanders or used as a political tool.

His work with Pershing advocating for such dramatic changes thrust Marshall into the world of Washington, D.C., politics. He met with legislators and policy makers to get their input and support. He was careful to maintain staunch political neutrality. Over the course of his career, he developed a stock answer as to which political party he supported: "My mother was a Republican, my father was a Democrat, and I'm an Episcopalian."

That Marshall presented himself as apolitical was not uncommon. By tradition, American soldiers have stayed neutral in politics, thus skirting the issue of military allegiance with a political party. Of course, the tradition is not always followed—a number of American presidents were once generals. But Marshall maintained the distinction between military service and politics. Over the course of his career, he would win respect from lawmakers of both parties.

Despite the sound arguments for UMT and the lobbying done by Pershing and his staff, the initiative ultimately failed to gain the support of Congress. Following the war, American lawmakers feared that creating a reserve of trained soldiers would lead to increased militarism at home. Having seen what a militant culture in the form of Prussian-dominated Germany could turn into, legislators and their constituents were hesitant to embark on any program to build up the military.

Pershing and his staff did manage to get some of their other proposals passed. Most notable was an effort to restructure the organization and number of military bases. The nation's network of army bases was still focused on the military realities of the 1800s, particularly the perceived threat that Native Americans posed to westward expansion. The outdated collection of army posts was exacerbated by pork barrel politics—legislators who sought to add or maintain military bases in their districts as a means of bringing in revenue and securing local jobs. Pershing hoped to reduce the number of these posts. This consolidation would save the army money and would reorganize troops in fewer, less far-flung bases that would make administering them easier.

Marshall's service under Pershing ended in 1924. In a farewell letter, he wrote, "My five years with you will always remain the unique experience of my career." In September of that year, Marshall, now a permanent lieutenant colonel after an August 1923 promotion, and his wife, Lily, sailed for China, where he was to serve

George Marshall at Fort Myer in Washington, D.C., in 1923. *(Courtesy of the George C. Marshall Foundation.)*

with the Fifteenth Infantry Regiment in Tientsin. It was not unusual for an officer's wife or family to accompany him to a new posting—just expensive.

In the early part of the 1900s, China was an unstable country, though one that still had a sizeable population of Western expatriates living there. After the Boxer

Uprising of 1898-1900, the revolution of 1911, and the successive counterrevolutions and power grabs staged by regional warlords, China lacked a real government. The United States, along with Britain, France, Italy, and Japan, occupied the country to provide order and police protection. While China was not an American protectorate like the Philippines, American troops were still present, acting as a safeguard against the sporadic fighting that persisted. In Tientsin, located just south of Peking (modern-day Bei-jing), Marshall commanded about a thousand men in an environment that did not constitute war but did not exactly constitute peace either.

Lily Marshall at the Tientsin railroad station in China, 1926. *(Courtesy of the George C. Marshall Foundation.)*

Although Marshall's troops never engaged in combat with the independent Chinese armies, they still had some harrowing times. Soon after Marshall's coming, rival warlords fought over the city of Peking. Opposing forces of perhaps 100,000 men spilled around Tientsin. Marshall's detachment was tasked with helping to safeguard the city by offering the Chinese soldiers food in exchange for their weapons. Their plan helped avoid further bloodshed. To express their gratitude for keeping the city safe from violence, the people of Tientsin bestowed upon Marshall and his regiment a marble gate that would later be brought back to Fort Benning.

The gate served as a tangible reminder of Marshall's impact while in Tientsin. But the most important thing nearly three years in China taught him was the importance of building morale among his troops. In China, as in his previous postings—especially those in the Philippines—there was not much for soldiers to do. Consequently his unit had become infamous for problems that arose out of boredom. Setting about to refocus his subordinates' off-hour proclivities for liquor and women toward something more constructive, Marshall developed athletic and recreational facilities and activities. He even created a sort of summer camp for the men and their families. Problems diminished and morale increased.

With another lesson learned and another country experienced, Marshall and Lily sailed for home in May 1927. George was on his way to a position at the Army War College, an institution which acted as a strategic-thinking finishing school for senior officers. There, others could benefit from the lessons he had learned in Filipino jungles, World War I planning sessions, and

Chinese garrisons. The move again put the Marshalls in Washington, D.C., still a relatively small government town.

Though the teaching position at the War College was a good one, it was not exactly an opportunity that Marshall wanted—he had turned down five previous requests from the school. While the Marshalls could have adjusted easily to Washington again, having already spent a number of years there and established routines and friendships, the transition was difficult. Lily's health had been surprisingly good while in China, but she became weak upon the return to the United States. In July, George began teaching. In August, Lily underwent surgery for a diseased thyroid gland and was slow to recover. Ultimately, George's assignment was cut short as Lily succumbed to the heart condition that had plagued her since childhood. She died on September 15, 1927.

FIVE

NEW BEGINNINGS

In October, following Lily's funeral, George took an assignment as the assistant commandant at the Infantry School at Fort Benning in Georgia. He was responsible for establishing the curriculum for the army's elite training center for younger infantry officers. The opportunity was rewarding because he was finally implementing ideas he had been thinking about for years. In addition, the engaging work helped him to offset some of the grief and loneliness that he had been feeling since Lily's death. He said the new posting provided "an unlimited field of activity, delightful associates, and all outdoors to play in. . . . The change to Benning was magical."

For the next five years, Marshall remained at Benning. He became a major force in the education of a class of commanders that would soon enough be called upon to lead. In the process he would alter the very idea of teaching in the army.

By the time he arrived at Fort Benning, Marshall had already had a number of experiences in the realm of teaching and instructing soldiers. These included his formal instructor's position at Leavenworth, stints training National Guard and volunteers before WWI, and further troop preparation during the war. As had been his calling card in these previous assignments, Marshall used his role as head of the academic department to implement his philosophy about teaching warfare and turned Benning into a first-class military school.

What he found when he arrived was an institution that was stuck in the past. Teachers were not up-to-date. Traditional lecture-based classes did not engage students, who were not encouraged to discuss issues or to question their teacher or each other. Theory and book-

During Marshall's five-year tenure at Fort Benning, the school underwent substantial modernizations, and by the 1940s, when this panoramic photograph of the fort was taken, Benning was one of the most sophisticated military schools in the country. *(Library of Congress)*

learning were the norm; in contrast, Marshall always favored practical, real-life examples.

Marshall sought to slowly but surely chip away at what he didn't like while instituting new practices and recruiting staff. In a conservative culture that resisted change, Marshall knew that acting too fast would alarm those around him and make change more difficult. But he was willing to take intermediate steps to get to a bigger goal. In order to get the right man to head the school's Tactical Section, he held the job open for a year until Joseph W. Stilwell (whom he knew from his assignment in China) could accept it. Eventually, Marshall managed to introduce a curriculum that challenged students to think and to innovate, particularly in realistic battlefield situations. For instance, rather than give his students accurate, up-to-date maps of the terrain around which they would be asked to devise a strategy, Marshall preferred to give the army's future commanders outdated maps or rough sketches—resources that would more realistically mimic what would be available to a battlefield commander. Ultimately, this would prove to be good practice, as WWII commanders—particularly those in the Pacific islands and in North Africa—would be lucky to have even a colonial-era map on which to base crucial decisions.

In one notable case, wanting to underscore the importance of always being aware of one's surroundings, Marshall gave his students a pop quiz with a single question: sketch the terrain of the walk they took to class.

The era between World War I and II was a crucial one in the development of warfare technology. The B-17 bomber, a plane that would play a significant role in World War II, was developed during this time. *(Library of Congress)*

Marshall's curriculum also placed the importance on staying abreast of emerging technology. He managed to get a number of tanks assigned to Fort Benning so that students could interact with the new reality of warfare. Marshall had also recognized the growing importance of warplanes but had to make do with only an annual demonstration rather than his own detachment of planes. Indeed, both tanks and planes symbolized how much technology had leapt forward. Such drastically improved—and more deadly—weapons meant that the way battles were fought would need to change; planning for war and training foot soldiers and officers needed to change as well.

Marshall's new approach to teaching involved student exchanges between the Infantry School at Benning and the Artillery School at Fort Sill. With its long-range, high-impact guns, artillery was often charged with "softening up" enemy targets with barrages of heavy explosive shells before infantry troops attacked with lighter, more mobile weaponry. Although both artillery and infantry needed the other to be successful, they had been traditional rivals. Marshall believed that exchanges between the schools would minimize that unhealthy rivalry.

In his classes, and in those of other instructors, Marshall replaced the traditional lecture format with a more casual, give-and-take exchange. Marshall explained, "I found it was many times more effective when a man talked off the cuff." The students welcomed these changes—though not necessarily the older faculty.

In a reminder of Marshall's own student days at Leavenworth under Major Morrison, his students at Benning began to think of themselves as "Marshall's Men." Their pride in being associated with Marshall and his new methods was justified; the students that came out of Fort Benning were a new breed of military leader.

As a result of five years of interactions with the students and staff of Fort Benning, Marshall had developed what was probably the army's most thorough list of outstanding commanders. Little did he know just how valuable this list would become.

Marshall's time at Fort Benning was not just a place to meet the future leaders of the army. In 1929, he accepted an invitation to dinner not far from the base.

It had been two years since Lily's death and Marshall was alone at the party when he met Mrs. Katherine Boyce Tupper Brown, a widow. After an enjoyable evening of conversation, George offered to drive Katherine home in his car.

Although the ride back should have only taken a few minutes, it lasted nearly an hour. When they finally arrived at the house where Katherine was staying, she remarked that it was odd that someone who had lived in the area for two years (and who had a passion for maps and knowing his surroundings) had such a hard time finding her house in such a small town.

Marshall slyly replied that it was in fact his thorough knowledge of the area that allowed him to drive around for so long, never passing her house, and thus giving the two of them more time to get to know one another.

When Marshall met Katherine he was very lonely. In addition to the death of Lily, his mother had passed away in October of 1928; his father in September 1909; and Lily's mother, with whom he had been close, in 1910.

In the spring of 1930, George Marshall, nearly fifty years old, and Katherine, two years younger, were engaged. They married in October in Baltimore. As a testament to the bond between Marshall and Black Jack Pershing, George's friend and mentor served as the best man. With his marriage to Katherine, George found himself a father for the first time. Katherine's children—Allen, Clifton, and Molly—were eleven, thirteen, and fifteen, respectively.

Marshall's second wife, Katherine Boyce Tupper Brown. *(Courtesy of the George C. Marshall Foundation.)*

As is often the way with blended families, it was a challenge for Katherine's children to fully accept a new father figure. Yet over time they developed a close relationship. Molly became Marshall's frequent horse-back-riding partner.

Marshall and his new wife took up their quarters at Fort Benning, where they would stay for just under two years before the army sent them off again. In June 1932, their next assignment came: Fort Screven, Georgia, where Lieutenant Colonel Marshall was to command the four hundred men of the Eighth Infantry. A year later, he would move north to take over as commander of Fort Moultrie, South Carolina.

Katherine Marshall recalled their arrival at Fort Screven: "Rather dilapidated after Benning, Fort Screven is on the coast, separated from Savannah by a ten-mile drive through the marsh lands, edged on either side by windblown palm trees and hibiscus plants."

While these posts were not glamorous, they did get Marshall back to actual troop command, something he continually longed for during his career. Writing to Pershing of his command at Fort Screven, he revealed how he preferred to be out with the troops versus performing his typical administrative and instructional

Windswept palms dot the sandy landscape of Fort Screven on Georgia's Tybee Island. *(Library of Congress)*

assignments, saying, "However small, it keeps me away from office work and high theory." Again his command was characterized by a focus on improving the everyday life and morale of the bases. Mindful as always of the relationship between the military and the civilian population, Marshall made an extra effort to establish good relations between his bases and the towns and people that surrounded them. In the early 1930s, the bond between the military and the civilian population was particularly strong because the army had been tasked with running the nation's network of Civilian Conservation Corps (CCC) camps.

Established in 1933 by President Franklin Delano Roosevelt, the CCC was created to provide jobs for some of the millions of Americans who were unemployed. Coming four years after the stock market crash of 1929, the CCC was part of Roosevelt's larger New Deal program, meant to combat the Great Depression that followed the stock market's collapse.

Calling on young men to engage in projects supporting reforestation, the CCC created hundreds of thousands of jobs in a short amount of time. It faced huge logistical issues. The government had to find and assign work, hire and train employees, and set up and administer the camps where the workers lived. As the CCC was, in structure and form, much like an army, the U.S. Army organized the camps.

At both Fort Screven and Fort Moultrie, it fell to Marshall to oversee CCC operations for his district, in addition to his regular duties. For Marshall and the CCC, this was a mutually beneficial arrangement. On one hand, the CCC gained a capable administrator who had considerable experience organizing vast amounts of people and equipment. After all, it was George Marshall who had spent years building the U.S. Army before and during World War I, and it was Marshall who had planned the Saint-Mihiel and the Meuse-Argonne offensives, two of the most stunning feats of logistical execution in the history of warfare. Marshall himself gained additional experience in mobilizing huge quantities of men and organizing assignments and supplies. But once again, Marshall's talents worked against him.

The Illinois National Guard requested that Marshall be transferred to their post in the position of senior instructor. The unit was in need of a good leader. High unemployment in the Chicago area could lead to rioting, in which case an organized and prepared National Guard would be needed in a hurry.

Considering his experience, Marshall was a perfect pick for the job, but it was not one that he wanted. The position would be a step backwards in his career. Although he had been promoted to full colonel in September, he was now nearly fifty-three and rapidly approaching retirement without having won a general's star or having made his mark on the army. Writing to a friend, he complained: "I deplore the fact that I have not gained a position of sufficient power to do what I think should be done. I am awfully tired of seeing mediocrity placed in high positions, with brilliance and talent damned by lack of rank to obscurity."

Marshall generally thought it unseemly to appeal to influential friends in order to get a favor. His apolitical stance was one of the traits that others found most appealing about him. Similarly, Marshall looked down on those who devoted time to promoting their own accomplishments as well as those who came to him asking for favors or to peddle influence. In many ways Marshall was the prototypical good soldier who believed in well-disciplined troops who followed orders. Therefore one can appreciate just how dire Marshall's situation was when it forced him to break his own code of conduct. After getting the news about the assignment in Illinois, Marshall went all the way to the top and appealed for help from the head of the army, chief of staff General Douglas MacArthur.

MacArthur, a contemporary of Marshall's, was an army superstar who won advancement early through distinguished commands in World War I and became the youngest chief of staff in the nation's history. General MacArthur did not intervene on Marshall's behalf. In fact, he noted that the lower-ranking Marshall was an ideal fit for the position, saying, "He has no superior among Infantry colonels."

Thus, in October 1933, Marshall began what would be a three-year assignment with the Illinois National Guard. In later years, MacArthur's lack of sympathy for Marshall's request—among many other real and perceived incidents between the two men during World War II and finally during the Korean War—would fuel talk of a bitter feud between the two soldiers.

Upon their arrival in Chicago, Katherine noted that George "had a grey, drawn look, which I have never seen before, and have seldom seen since."

In the end, Marshall made the best of this assignment. He became active in the business and social community in Chicago through his Guard contacts and even spoke at social gatherings. These contacts and experiences would be of great assistance to him later as he lobbied the industrial community to mobilize for war production before and during World War II. As he had from his other varied positions over the years, Marshall gained experience and insight that would prove valuable in the future.

After thirty-four years in the army, Marshall at last received his first star. On October 1, 1936, George C. Marshall was promoted to brigadier general and given command of the Fifth Brigade of the Third Division—as well as the regional CCC camps—located at Vancouver Barracks, Washington.

Marshall, shortly before receiving his first general's star.

Having called ahead to the barracks to say that he did not want a celebration for his arrival, Marshall was a bit chagrined to be welcomed by a band. Yet it was the exuberant greeting given to him at the gate by his dog, Pontiac, which was most rewarding. Said Katherine Marshall, "A welcome from his dog meant more to George Marshall than any formal reception that could have been given him."

At nearly fifty-six, Marshall's career was just starting to take off. The next fifteen years would keep him far busier than he had been as a young man. As if to underline the fact that Marshall was growing older, it was not long after his new promotion that he went to San Francisco for a thyroid operation.

Now a general, Marshall anxiously figured his chances of being promoted to his ultimate goal: chief of staff of the army. As chief of staff, he would be able to tackle the issues he had seen at his various posts around the world and raise the army out of its mediocrity. To be considered for the job, he was required to have four years of service left before mandatory retirement. Marshall just made this cutoff.

A little more than a year and a half after taking command of Vancouver Barracks, it looked as if Marshall was indeed on his way to the top. From Washington state to Washington, D.C., he was transferred to serve as assistant chief of staff in the War Plans Division of the War Department. Once again, the Marshalls packed up to move to Washington, D.C., in July 1938.

The War Department, now known as the Old Executive Office Building, is located adjacent to the White House in Washington, D.C. *(Library of Congress)*

The department to which Marshall was assigned was tasked with developing potential military scenarios (and possible military solutions) that might one day confront the United States. This preemptive planning had gone on long before Marshall arrived and would go on without him. Crafting plans is a major responsibility of the military, not just in war but in peace as well.

When Marshall reported for work, the responsibilities of the office were far from abstract. In 1938, war was very much on the minds of American citizens and military planners alike. Storm clouds of conflict were gathering over Japan in one hemisphere, and over Germany and the rest of Europe in the other. It was becoming apparent that the peace established by the Treaty of Versailles, which had concluded WWI, was falling apart.

Adolf Hitler and his Nazi Party enjoyed rising popularity in Germany during the 1930s. *(Library of Congress)*

Wrecked by a war that had ruined its industry, taken the lives of many of its people, and subjected it to costly punitive reparations, Germany faced terrible economic conditions. Its people were looking for hope. They found it in the form of Adolf Hitler. As head of the National Socialist German Workers' Party—otherwise known as the Nazi Party—that swept into power in 1933, Hitler vowed to rebuild Germany. His repressive government was filled with nationalistic bluster that blamed much of the country's ills on Jews and Communists.

As Hitler was consolidating his power through the 1930s, civil war broke out in Spain from 1936-1939.

Under General Francisco Franco, and aided by Germany and Italy, the Nationalists overthrew the government and established a repressive regime. Similarly, in Italy, Benito Mussolini and his Fascist Party had come to power in 1922, establishing yet another troubling state in Europe. As civil war

A fascist propaganda poster from the Spanish Civil War.

raged in Spain, Mussolini marched his troops into Ethiopia.

Back in the United States, only four months after starting in the War Plans Division, Marshall was reassigned—and, in a manner of speaking, promoted—to the position of deputy chief of staff under chief of staff Malin Craig in October of 1938. (Craig had succeeded MacArthur in 1935.) Though Marshall's chances of becoming the next chief of staff were good, he knew the clock was ticking. The next time the job opened up would be his one and only shot at the post to which he had aspired for so many years.

SIX

CHIEF OF STAFF

On September 1, 1939, the *New York Times* proclaimed: "German Army Attacks Poland." A blurb on page eight of the next day's paper made mention of another event from the previous day: General George C. Marshall was sworn in as the new chief of staff of the United States Army.

A year earlier, in October 1938, the leaders of Britain and France met with Germany's leader, Adolf Hitler, in Munich. In an attempt to avoid another European war, Hitler was allowed to occupy the Sudetenland and to retain control of Austria in return for a promise to stop his advances. After the Munich meeting, in one of history's more famous misstatements, British prime minister Neville Chamberlain returned to England and proclaimed that the leaders had achieved "peace for our time."

A few months later, German troops occupied all of Czechoslovakia, and Italy took Albania. France and Great Britain gave up any hope for peace and began to prepare for war. In response, Germany and Italy signed an alliance, and the Soviet Union made a nonaggression pact with Germany. On September 1, 1939, German tanks rolled into Poland. Britain and France declared war two days later.

The Germans conquered Poland by employing a huge, well-trained modern army with new equipment that rapidly swept over their adversaries. This new military strategy relied heavily on the massive speed and power

The German invasion of Poland on September 1, 1939, marked the beginning of World War II.

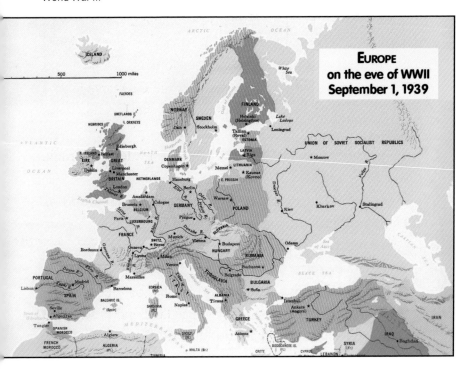

General Marshall *(center)* being sworn in as the chief of staff of the army on September 1, 1939. Secretary of War Harry H. Woodring stands to the left and the Adjutant General Major General Emory S. Adams stands to the right. *(U.S. Army Signal Corps Photo / Library of Congress)*

afforded by mechanized fighting units (composed largely of armored vehicles, troop trucks, and tanks) and was known in German as *blitzkreig*—"lightning war." For those in Paris, London, and Washington, D.C., it was both awe inspiring and terrifying.

Writing to the former chief of staff, Malin Craig, a few days after his recent promotion and the simultaneous beginning of World War II, Marshall quipped, "I think you timed your affairs very beautifully because you certainly left me on a hot spot."

In actuality, Marshall had secured the appointment in April and had been serving as the acting chief of staff for two months before formally assuming control of the army. He was well prepared for the job, even though some worried that he lacked frontline experience. Marshall's stellar record and reputation outweighed that concern.

In an interview with President Franklin D. Roosevelt held before he was offered the job, Marshall was his usual professional but blunt self. Reminiscent of his dramatic encounter with Pershing on the training grounds in France, Marshall recalled telling the president that if he were given the job of chief of staff, he wanted the right to say what needed to be said, even if the news was unpleasant. When Roosevelt agreed, Marshall belabored the point, saying, "You said yes pleasantly, but it may be unpleasant." Marshall was intent that his position be as independent as possible. He insisted that the affable and personable Roosevelt address him by his military title.

Despite clear indicators that Nazi Germany posed a very real threat to Europe, including American allies France and Britain, the mood on the American home front remained isolationist. There were many who felt that the United States had been tricked into WWI—at a cost of more than 100,000 American lives. To these Americans, Europe was a world away. In the spring of 1940, a Gallup Poll noted that more than 40 percent of the country thought sending aid to Britain and France was a mistake and would lead to American involvement in the war. On the other side, the so-called interventionists feared that the collapse of the Western European democracies in 1940, which left only Great Britain to stand between German aggression and the United States, placed the United States in grave peril. If Britain were defeated, Hitler would turn his sights on America. They argued the United States should go to war against the Axis powers (Germany, Italy, and Japan) to prevent Britain from falling, instead of remaining neutral until it was too late.

Marshall was among those who hoped America could stay out of the war. However, he was also realistic about the likelihood that the United States would be forced to fight. He set about to make the army ready. There was much to do.

The U.S. Army ranked seventeenth in the world as a military power. Marshall described the state of the army in this way: "On July 1, 1939, the active Army of the United States consisted of approximately 174,000 enlisted men scattered over 130 posts, camps, and stations . . . Within the United States we had no field army. There existed the mere framework of about 3½ square divisions approximately 50 per cent complete . . . As an army we were ineffective. Our equipment, modern at the conclusion of the World War, was in large measure obsolescent. In fact, during the postwar period, continuous paring of appropriations had reduced the Army virtually to the status of that of a third-rate power."

In contrast to the three and a half incomplete divisions—each representing a force of about 15,000 men—the Germans at this time had ninety combat divisions, the Japanese had fifty in China alone, and the Italians had forty-five. Each division might represent 20,000-30,000 men. America was greatly outnumbered.

For Marshall it was like a recurring bad dream. He had been at the heart of the effort to prepare American forces for battle in WWI, when it had taken more than a year to get forces into battle. Following WWI, it was clear to the military and political leaders that America must be better prepared for future conflicts. Under Pershing, Marshall spent years advocating a system that would help.

Yet the army in 1939 and 1940 was in much the same position as it had been twenty-five years earlier because the recommendations to maintain a larger army or to institute Universal Military Training had been rejected. The army that Marshall inherited as chief of staff was once again small and unprepared for battle. It lacked modern weapons and equipment, notably adequate stocks of airplanes, tanks, and other mechanized vehicles.

The outlook in Europe was bleak. In the spring of 1940, Germany took Denmark, Norway, the Netherlands, and Belgium. At the end of June, France fell. The secretary of the treasury, Henry Morgenthau, and Marshall resolved to meet with President Roosevelt

President Franklin D. Roosevelt, under whom Marshall served as the army's chief of staff.

about the urgent need to spend money to get the country ready for war. Morgenthau had a closer relationship with the president than Marshall, so it was agreed that he would do the talking. But Roosevelt was not convinced by his treasury secretary's words. Morgenthau asked if Roosevelt would listen to Marshall. The president replied, "I know exactly what he would say. There is no necessity for me to hear him at all."

Controlling his anger and frustration, Marshall asked Roosevelt for three minutes to make his case. Roosevelt acquiesced, and Marshall made an impassioned plea for money, men, and equipment. He ended by saying, "If you don't do something . . . and do it right away, I don't know what is going to happen to this country."

The message got through. Roosevelt asked Congress for nearly a billion dollars for the military. Marshall became a well-recognized face on Capitol Hill as he met frequently with legislators and testified before Congress. He was respected for his straight talk and honest approach. However, securing funding was no easy task. Among voters, there was little support for military expenditures for foreign wars. The Depression meant that money at all levels was tight.

One of the biggest wins that Marshall and the army scored in the buildup to WWII was the passage of a selective service act, which instituted a draft, and the call-up of National Guard and reserve units in the summer of 1940. Traditionally, the National Guard was only used domestically and usually in situations in which lives or property had to be defended. Mustering them for what might be service overseas was controversial. Army reserve units were designed to make trained troops available quickly without the expense of a standing army. Calling them into active service reflected the administration's belief, the U.S. would soon be at war.

In October of 1940, more than sixteen million men between twenty-one and thirty-six registered for the draft and were assigned a number. On October 30, 1940, Secretary of War Henry Stimson, blindfolded with a piece of cloth taken from one of the chairs used during the signing of the Declaration of Independence, proceeded to draw out numbers from a bowl. If one's number was picked, he was called for duty. Though the actual wording of the selective service bill provided for longer mandatory service if a national emergency existed, the predominant understanding was that "being drafted" required a single year of service. In 1940, some 18,000 men were inducted into service; a year later it was more than 900,000, and in total the system would induct more than ten million men into service during World War II.

The draft meant that the army could finally start to fill the gaps in its units. Marshall, however, knew that it would be months before the military was ready. There was a hope among military leaders—particularly in the

This draft card, issued in 1942, is from the 4th Draft, nicknamed the Old Man's Draft. It required mandatory registration for all U.S. men aged 45 to 64. Although the men would most likely not see military duty, they would be available for work in industries supporting the war effort. *(National Archives)*

REGISTRATION CARD—(Men born on or after April 28, 1877 and on or before February 16, 1897)

SERIAL NUMBER — U 1442 — 1. NAME (Print) Minka Johnson Habben — ORDER NUMBER

2. PLACE OF RESIDENCE (Print) R. 4. Carthage Hancock Illinois

1. MAILING ADDRESS SAME

4. TELEPHONE — 5. AGE IN YEARS 60 — 6. PLACE OF BIRTH Hancock

DATE OF BIRTH 11 11 81 — Illinois

7. NAME AND ADDRESS OF PERSON WHO WILL ALWAYS KNOW YOUR ADDRESS Mrs. Ijode Habben

8. EMPLOYER'S NAME AND ADDRESS Self

9. PLACE OF EMPLOYMENT OR BUSINESS Carthage Hancock Ill.

I AFFIRM THAT I HAVE VERIFIED ABOVE ANSWERS AND THAT THEY ARE TRUE.

Minka Habben

D. S. S. Form 1 (Revised 4-1-42) (over)

offices of Marshall and Admiral Harold R. Stark, the chief of naval operations—that if war was going to come, let it come later. Marshall was working against the clock, scrambling to raise adequate men and equipment. Yet at the same time, as the draftees were folded into the army without a war to fight, there was mounting pressure to discharge them sooner.

Even though he was one of the most accomplished army-builders in the country—if not the world—Marshall still struggled to convert millions of civilians into a formidable army. At even the most basic level there were problems. One of the loudest complaints made by draftees (and their parents, elected officials, and the media) was that even though the army had been begging for new recruits, it had nowhere to put them. There was a housing shortage for soldiers, as the barracks and bases from WWI had fallen into disrepair.

At the root of many of Marshall's problems was a military bureaucracy that had not functioned efficiently for years. Two decades after the end of WWI, the army and the War Department were mired in inefficient management structures, overlapping jurisdictions, time-consuming red tape, and general lethargy. Marshall had once been given a form to sign in order to account for a twenty-eight-dollar property loss. His signature was required in twelve different places and he counted nearly thirty other names on the form.

During a cold winter at Fort Benning, troops did not have adequate housing and had not been sent warm clothes and blankets. Marshall gave orders to resolve the situation but a few weeks later discovered that the soldiers were still without their warm clothes because the request was held up in red tape. Marshall could show flashes of rage and this was one of those times. He ordered, "Get these blankets and stoves and every other damn thing that's needed out tonight, not tomorrow morning, not two weeks from now. I don't care what regulations are upset or anything of that character. We are going to take care of the troops first, last, and all the time."

About his bold plan for economic recovery called the New Deal, President Roosevelt declared, "Take a method and try it. If it fails, admit it frankly and try another. But above all, try something." Similarly, Marshall entreated those who worked for him to take action. The chief of staff would constantly tell his subordinates to make things happen; he could forgive them for taking the wrong action, but inaction was inexcusable. Still, it was clear that the problem was in the army's cumbersome organization, rules, and regulations. The whole bureaucracy would need to be changed to cope with wartime demands.

Marshall's efforts to change the system depended on changing the people. This forced him to make a number of tough decisions, relieving officers—some of them old friends—of their commands in favor of others who would do their jobs better. This bloodletting produced significant enmity.

Changing people also meant tapping a new generation of military leaders. Marshall's ability to pick gifted men was extraordinary. Perhaps the thing that American army commanders feared most was getting on George Marshall's unfavorable list. Over the course of his years in the army, he had kept his eyes and ears open, noting which soldiers would make good officers.

Although his time as an instructor at Fort Benning had been a gold mine for discovering highly capable officers, Marshall also relied on the results of practice maneuvers to get a sense of which soldiers would make good leaders. The grandest of these war games occurred in September of 1941 across thousands of square miles in Louisiana and Texas and involved nearly a half mil-

Major General Lesley J. McNair briefs General Marshall during the practice maneuvers in Louisiana in September of 1941. *(Combined Arms Research Library, Leavenworth, Kansas)*

lion men. The maneuvers were a proving ground not only for the new recruits, new equipment, and new techniques—including assaults using paratroopers—but they also were the best gauge that Marshall had to determine how the top officers would fare in a large-scale, rapidly changing battle.

Congress complained about the cost of mounting these exercises, but Marshall contended that they were well worth it: "I want the mistake down in Louisiana, not over in Europe, and the only way to do this is to try it out, and if it doesn't work, find out what we need and make it work."

Bucking tradition again, Marshall placed an emphasis on promoting enlisted men to positions of leadership; often these men were good leaders who did not have the resources to go to college and become commissioned officers via that route. Not only was Marshall trying to build a better army but, as had been his habit throughout his career, he was also a proponent of nurturing the careers of capable young soldiers. Having been a very talented junior officer whose career stalled because of an antiquated promotion system, Marshall sympathized with young, talented officers and did his best to reward their abilities.

To get these men into positions where their talents could benefit the army, the chief of staff cared little about a soldier's length of service. In one notable example, Marshall was impressed by Dwight D. "Ike" Eisenhower's performance in practice maneuvers and his reputation with other officers. Consequently, Marshall promoted Eisenhower over 350 more senior candidates. He did the same with other young officers—including George Patton and Omar Bradley—who became celebrated leaders.

Even after replacing the deadwood in the ranks, the entire army bureaucracy still needed to be restructured. When Marshall took over as chief of staff, his department consisted of 122 men—far from the multitudes that would later become part of the military command organization. Just because the staff was small, though, did not mean that it was efficient.

In 1941, it was estimated that there were at least sixty officials from the army and War Department who had direct access to the chief of staff. Marshall assigned a group to drastically overhaul the system so that, in the end, only six people reported directly to him.

Not only did the group come up with a revamped system to restructure the army, often eliminating posts or entire departments, but Marshall also put in place a "plucking committee" to remove unfit leaders from the ranks. This committee of retired officers, including former chief of staff Malin Craig, had a mandate to identify the worst senior officers and eliminate them in order to get better, younger officers up through the ranks. The committee removed nearly two hundred officers in its first six months and would remove hundreds more by war's end. These were all men who had spent years, often entire careers, in the army; suddenly they found themselves dismissed. Many of these men had connections to people in government and the press whom they would beseech to defend their livelihoods.

Businesslike and methodical—some said ruthless—Marshall's changes incurred tremendous ill will in an organization accustomed to the status quo. Yet Marshall believed that the changes had to be made. Ineffective leaders and bad processes that might be harmless in peacetime could cost lives and the country victory in war.

As Marshall was fighting to restructure the army and to gain funding from a reluctant Congress, other battles were being fought elsewhere in the world.

After the fall of Belgium, the Netherlands, and France in 1940, Great Britain was the only nation that stood between the Germans and total victory in western Europe. Instead of invading the island nation, Hitler relied on his air force, the Luftwaffe, to bomb it into submission. Much to Hitler's surprise, the British refused to surrender. Under the inspiring leadership of Prime Minister Winston Churchill, it eventually became evident to the Germans that the only way to defeat Great Britain would be by

British prime minister Winston Churchill.

invasion. Crossing the English Channel and making an amphibious landing on the English coastline would be a dangerous and expensive undertaking for Germany.

Hitler had been able to focus on the western front because of the treaty he had made with dictator Joseph Stalin of the Soviet Union in 1939. Russia had taken advantage of the war and the treaty to invade and seize parts of Poland, the Baltic states of Estonia, Latvia, and Lithuania, and to extend its influence in Finland. Denmark and Norway were under German control by the summer of 1940.

Hitler had long considered the communist Soviet Union to be his principal enemy in Europe. He believed Germany had a strong claim to Poland and most of Russia. As it became apparent that Great Britain was not going to surrender, Hitler decided to begin what he had always intended to be the second phase of his conquest of Europe. On June 22, 1941, German troops launched a massive attack into Soviet territory. The Soviet Union was caught unprepared, and for the first weeks, the Germans were able to sweep almost unimpeded across the vast plains of the western Soviet Union. The German advance finally ground to a halt the first week of December 1941, only miles from the city limits of the Soviet capital of Moscow.

Despite pleas for help from the British and the knowledge that war would likely spread to America if Britain fell, many Americans were still determined to stay out of the war. After all, America had not been attacked.

Firefighters in London struggle against overwhelming flames after a bombing during the Blitz in 1941. *(National Archives)*

During the darkest days for Great Britain, when nightly bombing rates were destroying huge parts of London and other major cities, and thousands of civilians were dying, President Roosevelt looked for ways to come to their aid while maintaining technical neutrality. Speaking on December 29, 1940, in one of his fireside chats, Roosevelt laid out his defense for American support of the British, saying:

> Some of our people like to believe that wars in Europe and in Asia are of no concern to us. But it is a matter of most vital concern to us that European and Asiatic war-makers should not gain control of the oceans which lead to this hemisphere.... If Great Britain goes down, the Axis powers will control the continents of Europe, Asia, Africa, Australia, and the high seas— and they will be in a position to bring enormous military and naval resources against this hemisphere.

It is no exaggeration to say that all of us, in all the Americas, would be living at the point of a gun—a gun loaded with explosive bullets, economic as well as military. . . . As planes and ships and guns and shells are produced, your Government, with its defense experts, can then determine how best to use them to defend this hemisphere. The decision as to how much shall be sent abroad and how much shall remain at home must be made on the basis of our overall military necessities. We must be the great arsenal of democracy.

In March of 1941, Roosevelt convinced Congress to pass the Lend-Lease Act, which allowed Great Britain to buy materials from the United States without having to pay in hard currency. For example, America received the use of British naval bases as payment for American destroyers. Such measures created loopholes in America's technical neutrality and brought on the ire of those who thought it provoked German aggression.

Still, American leaders did not declare war. As a result, there were frequent calls to discharge American draftees who would soon be nearing a year of service in September of 1941. Both Marshall and Roosevelt knew that if the soldiers that had been trained in the last year were to be discharged, the army would be no better off than it had been. Seeking to avoid this, Roosevelt declared a national military emergency that extended the service of the trained soldiers. The decision was not popular.

SEVEN

WAR

As 1941 neared its close, Marshall and most other leaders realized it was only a matter of time before the United States would be drawn into the worldwide conflict. However, they were not prepared for how it happened.

At 7:53 AM on December 7, 1941, the whine of propeller-driven planes broke the otherwise calm Sunday morning on the Hawaiian island of Oahu, home of the U.S. Pacific Fleet at Pearl Harbor. The peaceful morning erupted into pandemonium as waves of Japanese bombers laid waste to the unsuspecting American fleet. Launched from aircraft carriers less than three hundred miles from the Hawaiian coast, the Japanese bombers left death and destruction in their wake: 2,403 dead, 164 planes destroyed and nearly as many damaged, and eight battleships and another ten ships either destroyed or heavily damaged. America's Pacific Fleet, its major threat to deter Japanese aggression in the Pacific, was badly weakened.

For months, relations between the United States and Japan had been steadily deteriorating. Overt signs of the crumbling relationship could be found in any newspaper—the *New York Times* of December 7, 1941, carried headlines reading "Joint Plans to Thwart Japan" and "Big Forces Are Massed For Showdown in Pacific." The U.S. government also had the benefit of being able to

The USS *West Virginia* and the USS *Tennessee* under fire during the attack on Pearl Harbor, December 7, 1941. *(National Archives)*

read secret Japanese messages thanks to code-breaking work done by American cryptographers. All signs pointed towards a Japanese surprise attack on U.S. territories. This method of drawing first blood seemed all the more likely considering the Russo-Japanese War (1904-1905) had begun with a Japanese surprise attack on the Russian fleet.

U.S. military planners—including Marshall—believed that the attack would most likely be on the Philippines. For this reason, Marshall and Admiral Stark had concentrated their efforts on reinforcing the Philippines rather than Hawaii. In July 1941, Marshall recommissioned MacArthur with command of the United States Army Forces in the Far East. Aside from being one of the military's most respected leaders, MacArthur was an expert on the Philippines and had influence in the strategic island chain. His principal assignment was to defend the Philippines; it seemed clear that a Japanese attack on the islands was imminent.

The Philippines were close to Japan, particularly when compared to more distant bases like Pearl Harbor. They would be an easier target for the Japanese to reach and they represented a more immediate threat to Japan, as American bombers stationed there could more easily threaten the Japanese islands.

In a directive sent to the Pacific commanders on November 24, 1941, Admiral Stark reported: "Chances of favorable outcome of negotiations with Japan very doubtful. This situation coupled with statements of [Japanese] government and movements of their naval and military forces indicate in our opinion that a surprise aggressive movement in any direction including attack on Philippines or Guam is a possibility. Chief of staff has seen this dispatch, concurs and requests action addressees to inform senior army officers in their areas. Utmost secrecy necessary in order not to complicate an already tense situation or precipitate Japanese action."

Three days later, Marshall sent a memo to Pacific commanders that said:

> Negotiations with Japanese appear to be terminated to all practical purposes with only the barest possibility that the Japanese Government might come back and offer to continue. Japanese future action unpredictable. But hostile action possible at any moment. If hostilities cannot repeat cannot be avoided the United States desires that Japan commit the first overt act. This policy should not repeat not be construed as restricting you to a course of action that might jeopardize your defense. Prior to hostile Japanese action you are directed to take such reconnaissance and other measures as you deem necessary. But these measures should be carried out so as not repeat not to alarm the civil population or disclose intent.

Some have seen the attack on Pearl Harbor as part of a conspiracy. It has been posited that Roosevelt and the military antagonized the Japanese, hoping they would make an attack and thereby grant the government free rein to conduct war. Historians and the congressional panel that looked into the events leading up Pearl Harbor eventually concurred that the statement "the United States desires that Japan commit the first overt act" was not meant to draw America into war. Rather, Marshall was trying to address how commanders could defend their bases and their men while still keeping in mind that the public would see an American strike as warmongering. Most historians agree the Japanese devastation of Pearl Harbor resulted from a combination of genuine surprise and military incompetence.

The list of what-ifs with Pearl Harbor is frustratingly long. What if American military planners had been less specific about their belief that a Japanese strike would be made first against the Philippines rather than Pearl Harbor? What if the radar operators who had picked up the Japanese attack as it approached had sounded an alert rather than believing it was a flight of friendly planes that was scheduled to arrive that day? What if the commanding army general had directed his forces the previous week to be on the alert for a full-scale attack rather than the sabotage raid for which he had prepared? What if intelligence agents had hit upon the importance of Japanese messages in the days before the attack? What if the latest update of deciphered intelligence to Pearl Harbor had been sent using the navy's radio equipment or that of Western Union and RCA, rather than the slower army relay network?

While the Japanese attack on Pearl Harbor handicapped America's ability to wage war, it had a profound

Organizations such as the Red Cross, the Civilian Defense Council, and the military saw a sharp rise in volunteer involvement after the bombing at Pearl Harbor. *(Library of Congress)*

effect on the American people. Shocked, scared, and angry, the sneak attack on Pearl Harbor galvanized a nation that, up until December 7, was deeply divided about the war. Pearl Harbor steeled America's resolve as perhaps no other event could have and fueled a burst of patriotism and a flood of volunteers into the army and navy. It also freed up substantial funds for the military and silenced those who were calling for the discharge of draftees.

The day after the attack, Roosevelt addressed Congress and the nation, asking for a declaration of war on Japan:

> Yesterday, December 7, 1941—a date which will live in infamy—the United States of America was suddenly and deliberately attacked by naval and air forces of the Empire of Japan. . . the Japanese Government also launched an attack against Malaya. Last night Japanese forces attacked Hong Kong. Last night Japanese forces attacked Guam. Last night Japanese forces attacked the Philippine Islands. Last night the Japanese attacked Wake Island. This morning the Japanese attacked Midway Island. . . . I believe I interpret the will of the Congress and of the people when I assert that we will not only defend ourselves to the uttermost but will make very certain that this form of treachery shall never endanger us again. . . . I ask that the Congress declare that since the unprovoked and dastardly attack by Japan on Sunday, December seventh, a state of war has existed between the United States and the Japanese Empire.

Later that day, Congress declared war on Japan, precipitating a declaration of war on the United States by Germany and Italy. Consequently, on December 11, Roosevelt again asked for a declaration of war, this time against Italy and Germany, writing: "The long known and the long expected has thus taken place. The forces endeavoring to enslave the entire world now are moving toward this hemisphere. Never before has there been a greater challenge to life, liberty, and civilization. Delay invites greater danger. Rapid and united effort by all the peoples of the world who are determined to remain free will insure a world victory of the forces of justice and of righteousness over the forces of savagery and of barbarism."

After years of anxious anticipation, the United States was now officially at war with three countries on opposite sides of the globe: Japan in Asia, and Germany and Italy in Europe.

Marshall had spent the last two years carefully preparing the army in the face of political resistance. Now his hands were untied, but there was little time left.

The attack on Pearl Harbor meant the United States would again go to war unprepared. The war would have at least two fronts: in Europe against Germany and Italy, and in Asia and the Pacific against Japan. The demand for supplies, equipment, and materiel far exceeded availability. Almost everything that could be produced— from boots to bullets to bombers—was needed immediately. This need extended beyond America's own troops to include the Allies: Britain and its Commonwealth countries (including Australia and New Zealand), Russia, China, the resistance armies of France and Belgium, and the governments of Central and South America, notably Brazil.

To create order, the American war effort had to be coordinated with its allies, especially the British. Two weeks after Pearl Harbor, President Roosevelt and Prime Minister Winston Churchill and their respective military advisors met in Washington, D.C., for the Arcadia Conference, which lasted from December 22, 1941, to January 14, 1942.

The most important decision was where to concentrate the fight first. In general, the two sides agreed that the initial focus should be on defeating the Axis powers in Europe. This strategy was referred to as "Europe-first" or "Germany-first." There were not enough resources to fight what amounted to two wars—one in Europe and one in the Pacific—at the same time. The Japanese were considered to be the lesser of the two threats, despite their attack on Pearl Harbor. It would be easier to take a defensive position in the Pacific, with all of its miles and miles of ocean that isolated combatants, until more military might could be concentrated there.

Marshall proposed an amphibious assault on occupied France from England—a quick trip across the Channel. In theory, the British liked the idea but they felt that Marshall's goal of launching the attack in 1942 was unrealistic. The British had been fighting since 1939 and dreaded the casualties the offensive might cause. Churchill and his military staff lobbied Roosevelt and the American military commanders to make an initial push into North Africa, secure the Mediterranean Sea, and control the Middle East oil fields first. This would secure British possessions, create a southern front as a possible alternate invasion route, and draw German forces away from the Soviet front where the Russians were beginning to have some success stopping German progress.

Both sides knew that some action had to be taken to prevent the enemy from solidifying its positions. It was also important to boost the morale of the Allied civilian and military populations that had been hearing about defeats and setbacks in movie newsreels and radio broadcasts.

It was hard for Marshall to agree to launch operations in North Africa and the Middle East. While the British had substantial national interests in the region, America did not. It would be difficult to get popular support for such an operation. Admiral Ernest J. King, the head of the U.S. Navy, and Douglas MacArthur were also pressuring Marshall to commit more forces to the Pacific.

MacArthur was the country's most celebrated military leader in 1942. After graduating first in his class at West Point, he won praise for his daring leadership during World War I—when Marshall was stuck behind a desk at headquarters—and then held a succession of high-profile jobs following the war. These included superintendent of the United States Military Academy and commander of the District of Manila, as well as the Fourth and Third Corps Areas and the Ninth Corps Area. In 1930, he became the youngest army chief of staff.

Having served as chief of staff until October 1935, MacArthur then became military adviser to the government of the Philippines and remained in this capacity even after retiring from active service in 1937. Considered both a great leader and a great tactician, MacArthur

General Douglas A. MacArthur.

was a colorful character. With his corncob pipe, leather jacket, and braid-encrusted general's cap, he was easily recognized—and he enjoyed the attention. Unlike Marshall, who was uncomfortable with self-promotion, MacArthur had a penchant for publicity and saw himself as a man of destiny bound for greatness, including, perhaps, the presidency.

George Marshall's huge list of important duties— coordinating military-industrial production and distribution, advising the president, determining strategy within the army, coordinating with the navy and the

Allies, working with Congress, and a host of other issues—were often complicated by the people with whom he had to work. Roosevelt, Churchill, MacArthur, and Admiral King did not always get along. Marshall had to struggle to forge consensus, if not agreement.

Admiral King was once kept waiting in Marshall's office because a previous meeting had run long. Angered by the delay, the short-tempered head of the navy, whom his daughter described as "always in a rage," stormed out. When Marshall heard about the incident, he went to apologize, knowing that it would be impossible to win the war if the two of them could not get along. Marshall explained: "We can't afford to fight. So we ought to find a way to get along together."

The Japanese had also attacked the Philippines on the same day they attacked Pearl Harbor. It soon became clear the Americans would not be able to hold off the superior Japanese forces there. Marshall ordered an evacuation; MacArthur insisted on staying and fighting with his men until the very end. Marshall finally convinced him that his death or capture would strike a heavy blow to American morale. Before he left, MacArthur famously proclaimed, "I shall return," promising to see the Philippines liberated from Japanese control. For MacArthur, defeating the Japanese was personal and he constantly pushed for more resources to be sent to the Pacific.

Marshall knew that if the United States and its allies were to win the war, they would need to establish a unified command structure: "I am convinced that there must be one man in command of the entire theater—air, ground, and ships. We cannot manage by cooperation. Human frailties are such that there would be emphatic unwillingness to place portions of troops under another service. If we can make a plan for unified command now, it will solve nine-tenths of our troubles."

Rather than have multiple commanders responsible for a theater of war, Marshall made the bold proposal that there be only one. Instead of having one top commander from the British army, the British navy, the American army, and the American navy, a single supreme commander would have control of both ground and naval forces from each country.

Marshall's plan made logical sense, but still met resistance, especially in the Pacific. Although the British had a number of interests in the area, including Hong Kong, Malaya, and Singapore, it was decided that the region should be under American command, as the United States had interests in the North American West Coast, Alaska, Hawaii, Guam, and the Philippines. Because most of the fighting would inevitably require significant naval support, it would have been logical for a naval commander to control the area with a unified army commander reporting to him. However, MacArthur far outranked every possible naval officer. The problem was that the navy refused to grant MacArthur control over their ships. This led to a rather unwieldy division of the Pacific theater into zones commanded by

General Eisenhower *(left)*, commander of the Allied armies in North Africa, and General Henri Honoré Giraud, commander of the French forces, salute the flags of both nations at Allied headquarters in Algiers, Algeria, in 1943. *(Library of Congress)*

MacArthur and Admiral Chester A. Nimitz.

In June 1942, Marshall sent Eisenhower to England to command American troops in Europe and to commence planning for both the North Africa and cross-Channel attacks. For the invasion of North Africa, Eisenhower selected General George S. Patton to lead the charge. Patton was one of the most colorful and difficult personalities with whom Marshall had to interact. A tank commander who had made his reputation with an aggressive style in practice maneuvers before the United States entered the war, Patton had been assigned to run the army's Desert Training Center. Independently wealthy, he had placed fifth in the Olympic pentathlon in 1912. He was also a gruff soldier nicknamed "Old Blood and Guts," who was known to spout

General George S. Patton in 1942. *(Library of Congress)*

obscenities and wore ivory-handled pistols in the fashion of a gunfighter. He had a passion for war and believed in reincarnation, convinced that in previous lives he had fought with the armies of Alexander the Great and Julius Caesar. Despite these eccentricities, there was no denying that Patton was a gifted tactician.

On November 8, 1942, after nearly a year's planning, the invasion of North Africa, code-named Operation Torch, began. The Allies landed more than 35,000 men on November 8, targeting Casablanca, Oran, and Algiers.

Both Eisenhower and Patton enhanced their reputations in North Africa. Patton gained lasting fame for his hard-charging tank assaults on the German Afrika Korps commanded by Field Marshal Erwin Rommel, the "Desert Fox." The advance buoyed Allied morale and proved that American and British army and naval units could work together effectively.

The tide slowly turned in the Allies' favor. The Germans were on the run in North Africa. In the Pacific, the

The battle of Midway in the Pacific.

fleet that had been crippled at Pearl Harbor was back in action and had inflicted much damage on the Japanese at the battle of the Coral Sea, May 7-8, 1942, and the more decisive American victory at the battle of Midway, June 3-6, 1942.

Still, the war was a long way from over. It would be several years before the horrors of Hitler's concentration camps were fully revealed. During the war, millions of Jews, as well as members of other ethnic groups the Nazis considered to be subhuman, would perish in an organized plan of annihilation so horrible the world would never be the same again.

EIGHT

OPERATION OVERLORD

By the time the Allies convened the Symbol Conference in January 1943, outside of Casablanca, Morocco, in North Africa, the American military was far different from the one that had started the war. As opposed to 174,000 soldiers in uniform in 1939, Marshall now oversaw a force of 5.4 million. German and Italian progress had been stopped in Europe and rolled back in Africa, as had the Japanese advance in the Pacific.

But for all the progress that had been made, there was deep disagreement about how to end the war. Again, Marshall pressed to invade France as early as possible, and the British continued to insist on attacking Europe from the south, via what Churchill called the "great prize" of Italy. Marshall's plan called for one massive operation that would deal a crippling blow to Germany.

Roosevelt *(front left)* and Churchill *(front right)* at the Symbol Conference in Casablanca in January 1943. George Marshall is standing directly behind Roosevelt. *(National Archives)*

This meant attacking well-fortified German positions in northern France and presumably taking heavy casualties. Churchill's approach allowed the Allies to advance in stages without pinning their success on one engagement.

After days punctuated both by uplifting reports from Eisenhower's forces in North Africa and fiery debates, the conference broke up. The Americans and the British had agreed that the priorities for the rest of the war should be to:

- Defeat Germany first and then focus on Japan.
- Smash the German U-boat campaign.
- Invade Sicily after North Africa was cleared of German troops.
- Bring Turkey into the war as an ally.

- Launch a combined bomber offensive (code-named Pointblank) to take out military targets, including U-boat construction yards and aircraft plants in Germany.
- Earn the unconditional surrender of Germany and Japan.

Marshall once again saw his plan to invade France put off—this time until the spring or summer of 1944. Believing that his invasion would end the war in Europe more quickly—although admittedly at a great cost—Marshall was frustrated by the delay. The Allies would spend more time fighting their way up through southern Europe while leaving the Germans lodged in France.

An invasion of Sicily was followed by the invasion of the Italian peninsula in September 1943. Marshall had known that, although the Italian army was weak, the mountainous terrain of Italy would pose deadly threats. River crossings and fighting in mountains and towns was bloody and difficult. Allied victory was inevitable, but it came at a high price.

While fighting raged in Italy, planning continued for Operation Overlord, the cross-Channel invasion of France. In August 1943, an Allied meeting was held to finalize plans. It was decided that Overlord would begin on May 1, 1944.

Marshall wanted to command the historic Overlord invasion that he had advocated for years. Since his earliest days at VMI, he had longed for a troop command—and this would be among history's most memorable battles.

Though it was controversial, the Allies eventually

agreed that the supreme commander for the operation should be American because the bulk of the invading troops would be American. For many, Marshall was the logical choice. As chief of staff, he had demonstrated brilliant strategy and planning skills, and had a unique ability to work with others. In addition, commanding Overlord would be Marshall's reward for his years toiling away in Washington, D.C.

President Roosevelt wrote to General Pershing, saying that giving Marshall the field command would make him, in the eyes of the public, "the Pershing of WWII." At the Casablanca Conference, Roosevelt spoke to Eisenhower, Marshall's only real competitor for the command: "Ike, you and I know who was Chief of Staff during the last years of the Civil War but practically no one else knows, although the names of the field generals . . . every schoolboy knows them. I hate to think that fifty years from now practically nobody will know who George Marshall was. That is one of the reasons I want George to have the big command—he is entitled to establish his place in history as a great General."

Others argued that giving Marshall the command was the wrong decision. Even Pershing wrote Roosevelt that "the suggested transfer of George Marshall would be a fundamental and very grave error in our military policy" for a number of reasons. Moving from the chief of staff to commanding one battle and one theater of war would be seen as a demotion. Marshall needed to stay in Washington, D.C., for the good of the Allied war effort.

He was irreplaceable in terms of his ability to oversee all the different theaters of the war and to work with Roosevelt, Churchill, and leaders from both the American and British armies and navies. Finally, many thought that it would be unwise to change the chief of staff midway through the war—it would take too long for someone else to become as knowledgeable.

Marshall soon displayed why he was so respected among his peers. Although he wanted the command, he was against self-promotion and had the best interests of the war effort foremost in mind. Not only did he not push for the command, he also insisted on remaining neutral when asked about it. In December 1943, Roosevelt finally asked Marshall point-blank if he wanted the Overlord assignment. Of the incident, Marshall recalled, "I just repeated again in as convincing language as I could that I wanted him to feel free to act in whatever way he felt was to the best interest of the country and to his satisfaction and not in any way to consider my feelings. I would cheerfully go whatever way he wanted me to go and I didn't express any desire one way or the other."

In the end, the president chose Eisenhower to lead Overlord. Marshall would remain in Washington and oversee the entire war effort. While he had gone out of his way to make Roosevelt feel comfortable about the decision, Marshall was disappointed, though he did not reveal his feelings. Roosevelt tried to soften the blow, saying to Marshall, "You know I do not think I could sleep well at night with you out of the country."

Years of planning finally came to a head on D-Day, June 6, 1944, when the Allied invasion force set off from England. It was an enormous undertaking: more than 150,000 men, 5,000 ships, and 11,000 airplanes. The invasion was extremely costly—the Allies suffered 10,000 casualties with more than 4,000 killed—but it literally put the United States and Britain on the road to Berlin and victory in Europe.

D-Day was stunning in its size and complexity. The beaches of France were heavily fortified by German defenses. Paratroopers had been dropped in behind German lines before the first wave of soldiers came ashore, but despite their efforts to subdue the defensive positions, the arriving Allied forces faced a fierce battle.

This 1944 painting by Joseph Gary Sheahan depicts the chaos of the landing at Omaha Beach during the D-Day invasion. *(U.S. Army Art Collection)*

Most of the casualties occurred in the first hours of the operation.

At the beginning of the war, Marshall would personally write condolence letters to the families of soldiers killed in action, but the staggering number of casualties soon meant his office could only send out engraved cards. Some found the gesture to be gracious while others felt that the cards were too impersonal. Marshall still wrote letters on occasion to convey his regret about the death of someone's husband, son, or father. He looked at the casualty lists on a daily basis and passed these on to Roosevelt so that they would not forget that decisions made in the safety of their offices in Washington, D.C., affected men thousands of miles away in the most profound way possible.

Sometimes the losses hit close to home. In May 1944, while serving in a tank unit in Italy, a sniper killed Marshall's stepson Allen. In July, errant U.S. bombs killed his good friend and colleague, Lieutenant General Lesley J. McNair.

Once the Allied troops had secured beach-landing zones, they moved into the French countryside. What became known as the Normandy campaign (named for the region of France) resulted in nearly half a million casualties before months of fighting freed France from German control. American and British forces then continued to advance towards Germany while the Soviets squeezed Hitler's armies on the eastern front. All over the world the Allies were making progress towards end-

American troops hold off the Germans in the Battle of the Bulge, the last major European conflict of World War II.

ing the war. The last major German offensive, the Battle of the Bulge, took place on December 16, 1944. It was repulsed and led to the eventual surrender of the German forces on May 8, 1945. Three days earlier, Hitler had committed suicide in a bunker in Berlin. Unfortunately, President Roosevelt did not live to see the end of the war. He died on April 12, 1945, of a cerebral hemorrhage. Vice President Harry Truman succeeded him.

Now, the focus turned towards Japan and the Pacific, as had been the plan from the start. Although the Allies had been steadily making gains, moving from island to island, Japanese resistance was fierce. Imbued with a fight-to-the-death spirit, Japanese forces inflicted large numbers of casualties by employing desperate suicide attacks and creating networks of tunnels that were difficult to overcome. The attack to take the island of Iwo Jima lasted four months and resulted in 26,000 American casualties. As a testament to Japanese ardor, most of the 20,000 defenders were killed in action—the Americans took only 218 prisoners. Similarly, fighting for the island of Okinawa lasted three months, cost 75,000 US casualties, and resulted in the stunning loss of 110,000 Japanese killed.

It was apparent that the Japanese would not surrender easily. To defeat the Japanese, it would be necessary to invade the home islands, with the goal of capturing Tokyo. It was obvious that such an invasion would result in a horrific amount of casualties on both sides.

General Marshall *(left)* confers with Colonel Thomas Harmon *(center)* and General Hap Arnold *(right)* after inspection of a B-29 Super Fortress at National Airport in Washington, D.C., on November 29, 1944. *(Library of Congress)*

A survivor of the atomic bomb stands among the utter ruins of Nagasaki days after the attack. *(AP Photo)*

Following years of secret work and a final test in July of 1945, the United States had developed a new weapon of tremendous magnitude: the atomic bomb. On August 6, one of these weapons was dropped over the Japanese city of Hiroshima, destroying 80 percent of the city and inflicting 130,000 casualties.

The Soviet Union declared war on Japan two days after the bombing of Hiroshima and quickly moved into Korea. The next day the United States detonated a second atomic bomb over the city of Nagasaki, with over 75,000 more casualties. A day later, the Japanese surrendered, ending World War II.

The decision to use atomic weapons—and to use them deliberately against the civilian population—was one that troubled policy makers at the time and has remained controversial. The argument usually made in favor of using the weapons is that, in the end, they saved lives—not only the lives of the American soldiers who would have died storming Japan but also the lives of the Japanese that would have been lost defending the home islands. However, the immediate impact of nuclear weapons is only part of the story behind their devastation. For years the effects of the bombings were felt as thousands of people who were not killed by the initial blast eventually succumbed to the aftereffects of radiation poisoning.

Looking at the problem from a military perspective, Marshall later said that he had no hesitation about using the nuclear option: "We had to end the war; we had to save American lives; we had to halt this terrific expenditure of money which was reaching a stupendous total. . . . The bomb stopped the war. Therefore, it was justifiable." Although Marshall, as a soldier and not a politician or statesman, was not as concerned with the political ramifications of the bombing, the bombs themselves were a political message sent partly to Japan and partly to the Soviet Union.

The war was finally over. In the midst of the joyous celebrations, Marshall deflected most attempts to heap awards upon him. Although he inevitably did have to accept a number of honors and endure much praise, he preferred to see others march in the parades and receive the thanks of a grateful nation and an appreciative world. He just wanted rest. By his own account, he had taken only nineteen days off since the war began and he wanted nothing more than to return

Crowds line Paris's Champs Élysées to view Allied tanks and half-tracks as they pass through the Arc de Triomphe after the French city was liberated from the Germans on August 25, 1944. *(Library of Congress)*

to Dodona Manor, his house in Leesburg, Virginia, to do some gardening and enjoy some much overdue rest and relaxation.

On November 26, 1945, Marshall resigned as chief of staff in favor of his protégé, Eisenhower. After more than forty-three years of service, Marshall said good-bye to his beloved army. Speaking at Marshall's retirement where he personally awarded Marshall his only decoration of the war—an Oak Leaf Cluster—Truman read the official citation: "In a war unparalleled in magnitude and horror, millions of Americans gave their country outstanding service. General of the Army George C. Marshall gave it victory." Churchill cited him as no less than the "organizer of victory." The world at peace, Marshall hoped to slip away into the retirement he so richly deserved.

NINE

COLD WAR

The Soviet Union was allied with the United States in World War II. However, in the final months of the war the relationship between the two countries became contentious. The Soviet Union, which had lost a staggering twenty million people, was determined to emerge as a world power and to exert dominance over Central and Eastern Europe and other parts of the globe. The U.S. was determined to thwart Soviet ambitions.

In March 1946—only six months after the Japanese surrender—Churchill crystallized the new global situation in a speech he delivered in President Truman's home state of Missouri:

> From Stettin in the Baltic to Trieste in the Adriatic, an iron curtain has descended across the Continent. Behind that line lie all the capitals of the ancient states

of Central and Eastern Europe . . . all these famous cities and the populations around them lie in what I must call the Soviet sphere, and all are subject in one form or another, not only to Soviet influence but to a very high and, in many cases, increasing measure of control from Moscow.

This tense world situation demanded the services of George Marshall. The day after his official retirement, Marshall was back in Leesburg enjoying his first day of freedom. His wife, happy to have him home and relaxed, went upstairs to take a nap. When she awoke, she turned on the radio to hear a breaking news story: George C. Marshall had just been appointed the U.S. ambassador to China.

Shocked, she went downstairs to tell her husband what she had just heard. George confirmed the news. President Truman had called and asked him to again come to the service of his country, and the obedient soldier had said yes. Thus began Marshall's second career as a statesman.

Writing to MacArthur, he noted dryly, "My retirement was of rather short duration."

China had been a vexing American problem for years, going back before Marshall's first assignment there in 1924. Two rival warlords, who had controlled China for years, were trying separately to unite the giant Chinese nation at the close of WWII, but friction was threatening to throw the country into civil war. The party nominally in control at the time of Marshall's arrival was the

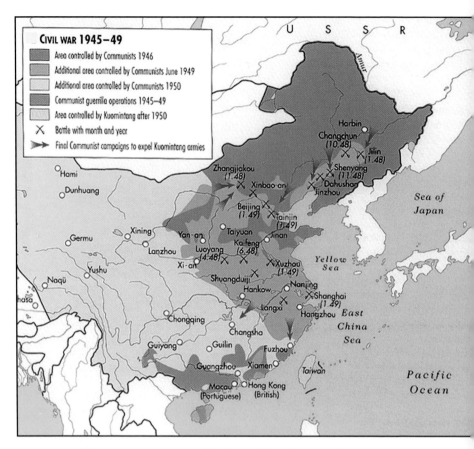

The primary areas of conflict from 1945-1949 during China's civil war.

Kuomintang, or Nationalist, Party headed by Chiang Kai-shek. The other party that had seen its power base rise in the waning years of WWII was the Communist Party of Mao Tse-tung.

The U.S. supported the Nationalists, although it had proclaimed official neutrality. Russia had fallen under Communist control in 1917, and many in the U.S. and Europe considered the ideology to be a grave threat to freedom and security. The poorer regions of the world, such as those in Asia, were feared to be fruitful ground for communism to take hold. While in reality communism had meant brutal dictatorship in the Soviet Union, the idea that all property and other forms of wealth should be owned by everyone equally could have strong appeal to people who had suffered under foreign control and corrupt dictators. Policy makers in the U.S., including President Truman, became convinced that communism had to be stopped, even if it meant war.

Despite this new, challenging postwar environment, most American politicians—to Marshall's chagrin— were eager to drastically shrink the size of the armed forces. Marshall feared that a smaller military and a national feeling of war-weariness opened up the door for the Soviets to expand their influence. With Japan ruined by the war and China near anarchy, a power vacuum existed that the Soviet Union was happy to fill. While the United States supported the Nationalists, the Soviet Union, not surprisingly, supported the Communists.

Marshall was asked to try to broker peace between the Nationalists and the Communists in China. Most considered it to be a nearly impossible task. It was hoped his reputation for being an honest broker close to the president gave him a chance of reconciling the two Chinese factions. In fact, Marshall did make progress. A cease-fire was announced, and American, Nationalist, and Communist representatives forged the framework for a coalition government. But Marshall was hampered by an American policy that required him to be a neutral mediator to both parties, while the U.S. government sup-

Marshall *(left)* converses with Nationalist party leader General Chiang Kai-shek and the Chinese general's wife during Marshall's visit to Nanking, China, in 1946. *(UPI / Bettmann Archive Photo)*

ported the Nationalists. In addition, there was such deep-seated distrust between the Communists and the Nationalists that reaching a common ground was impossible.

Writing to Eisenhower, he said of the situation, "My battle out here is never ending with both ends playing against the middle—which is me."

The situation was ultimately untenable. In January, after a year and more than three hundred meetings with the Chinese leaders, Marshall cabled to Truman that he could do no more and would return to the United States. In a matter of months, mainland China had fallen to the Communists, and the Nationalists fled to the island of Taiwan.

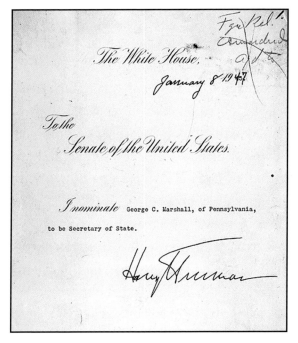

The White House,
January 8 1947

To the
Senate of the United States.

I nominate George C. Marshall, of Pennsylvania,
to be Secretary of State.

President Truman's nomination of Marshall as secretary of state. *(National Archives)*

After finishing his assignment in China, respite would be brief for the sixty-six-year-old general-turned-diplomat. One of the reasons Marshall returned from China was so President Truman could appoint him secretary of state. Marshall would become the president's chief advisor in foreign affairs. He would also assume the helm of the State Department, the agency responsible for formulating, representing, and implementing American foreign policy. Marshall was tasked with helping to create a global environment that would benefit Americans at home and abroad. However, because America had become the world's *de facto* leader—or at least co-leader along with the Soviet Union—the job of secretary of state expanded beyond looking out for American interests to looking out for the whole world. Instead of overseeing soldiers and military bases, Marshall would now be responsible for diplomats and embassies. Rather than worrying about supply lines, Marshall would now be concerned with diplomatic lines of communication.

Marshall had made his name building and rebuilding the army and winning a war. He was a man with strong bipartisan appeal who could be trusted. He had enormous personal prestige—he was one of only a handful of soldiers ever promoted to the five-star rank of General of the Army and was named *Time* magazine's Man of the Year in 1943, among other recognitions—which the State Department badly needed. But despite his years of interacting with the world's most powerful leaders, Marshall was not a diplomat. Regardless, Truman thought he could improve the morale and structure of the department.

Marshall oversaw America's foreign relations during one of the nation's most formative times. The iron curtain that Churchill described as descending between the Communist USSR and the United States and its Western allies had solidified. With the advent of nuclear weapons, the stakes were higher than ever.

At the end of the war, the United States was producing half of the world's goods and had unmatched economic and military supremacy. Europe had been ravaged by the war. Factories and infrastructure had been destroyed. Countries had incurred huge debts to keep their armies in the field. Men who otherwise would be farming, working in factories, or managing businesses were dead. Lack of economic vitality and jobs, enormous debt, and a sense of hopelessness created an environment of desperation that could very well ignite another major conflict.

There were massive problems to be faced. But first, Marshall set out to reform the State Department. He cut out the red tape he abhorred and, just as he had in the army, set out to find and install gifted subordinates. As a testament to his ability to pick good men, it is worth noting that two of his subordinates in the State Department, Dean Acheson and Dean Rusk, went on to become secretaries of state. Recalling the reforms that Marshall implemented, Acheson said, "I think for the first time in the history of the State Department, there was a line of command."

Marshall's work in improving the structure, organization, and personnel of the department won him kudos, but it was his international policy that would constitute the major part of his legacy in American history.

The Allies had created a Council of Foreign Ministers to iron out the particulars of the peace treaties with the various combatants. Composed of the chief statesmen of the United States, Great Britain, France, and the Soviet Union, the group met in London and Moscow in 1945 to decide issues regarding Japan and the Central European states, including how the countries' territories would be divvied up and administered. When Marshall

This painting, part of a triptych by Augustus Vincent Tack entitled *The High Command*, shows President Truman *(center left)* speaking with Marshall *(center right).* They are surrounded by *(from left to right)* Navy Fleet Admiral William D. Leahy, General Hap Arnold *(standing),* and Navy Fleet Admiral Ernest J. King. *(Courtesy of the National Portrait Gallery, Smithsonian Institution / Art Resource.)*

came on board as secretary of state, the ministers were set to convene in Moscow to discuss the conditions of the peace treaty with Germany and Austria.

In April 1947, after forty-three fruitless meetings, Marshall returned from the foreign ministers' confer-

ence convinced that forging a peace settlement was
impossible. The bad feelings between the U.S. and the
Soviets ran too deep. Marshall distrusted the Soviet
Union, as did others in the State Department. On February 22, 1946, George Kennan, a senior diplomat at the
U.S. Embassy in Moscow, crystallized what many were
already coming to believe: the Soviet Union should no
longer be thought of as America's friend and ally. America
needed to work to limit Soviet influence around the
world. Limiting Soviet influence was, on one hand, a
military question. Could the United States show that it
had the power to defeat the Soviets if they sought to make
war? On the other hand, much of the work of hampering
Soviet Communists was to keep them from making
economic and military allies.

This new U.S. policy toward the Soviet Union was
called containment. While Marshall was not the origi-
nator of the policy, it was under his watch that it was
adopted as a cornerstone of American foreign policy.
Containing the Soviets defined America's foreign policy
for nearly fifty years after Marshall left the Moscow
conference.

Only a month before Marshall returned from Moscow, President Truman had addressed a joint session of
Congress. On March 12, 1947, Truman threw down the
gauntlet, proclaiming America's new policy. Designed
with the Soviets in mind, the Truman Doctrine was a
dramatic break from American isolationism. The United
States promised to come to the aid of countries that

sought to fight off the influence of communism. Truman declared, "I believe that it must be the policy of the United States to support free peoples who are resisting attempted subjugation by armed minorities or by outside pressures."

Although Truman's words were sweeping, his immediate objective was more limited. The speech was meant to stir Congress to appropriate $400 million in aid to Greece and Turkey so the two countries could fight Communist rebels.

Within this context, it occurred to Marshall and the State Department that containing the Soviets and communism by leveraging America's economic resources, rather than using just military means, could benefit the United States and its allies. Speaking for a characteristically brief ten minutes at Harvard University on June 5, 1947, Marshall outlined a vision of economic assistance that was based on a simple idea: peace hinged upon economic prosperity. Conspicuous in his common civilian suit rather than graduation robes or a military uniform, Marshall presented the State Department solution:

> The truth of the matter is that Europe's requirements for the next three or four years of foreign food and other essential products—principally from America— are so much greater than her present ability to pay that she must have substantial additional help or face economic, social, and political deterioration of a very grave character.

The remedy lies in breaking the vicious circle and restoring the confidence of the European people in the economic future of their own countries and of Europe as a whole. The manufacturer and the farmer throughout wide areas must be able and willing to exchange their product for currencies, the continuing value of which is not open to question.

Aside from the demoralizing effect on the world at large and the possibilities of disturbances arising as a result of the desperation of the people concerned, the consequences to the economy of the United States should be apparent to all. It is logical that the United States should do whatever it is able to do to assist in the return of normal economic health in the world, without which there can be no political stability and no assured peace. Our policy is directed not against any country or doctrine but against hunger, poverty, desperation, and chaos. Its purpose should be the revival of a working economy in the world so as to permit the emergence of political and social conditions in which free institutions can exist. Such assistance, I am convinced, must not be on a piecemeal basis as various crises develop. Any assistance that this Government may render in the future should provide a cure rather than a mere palliative. Any government that is willing to assist in the task of recovery will find full cooperation, I am sure, on the part of the United States Government. Any government which maneuvers to block the recovery of other countries cannot expect help from us. Furthermore, governments, political parties or groups which seek to perpetuate human misery in order to profit therefrom politically or otherwise will encounter the opposition of the United States.

It is already evident that, before the United States Government can proceed much further in its efforts to alleviate the situation and help start the European world on its way to recovery, there must be some agreement among the countries of Europe as to the requirements of the situation and the part those countries themselves will take in order to give proper effect to whatever action might be undertaken by this Government. It would be neither fitting nor efficacious for this Government to undertake to draw up unilaterally a program designed to place Europe on its feet economically. This is the business of the Europeans. The initiative, I think, must come from Europe. The role of this country should consist of friendly aid in the drafting of a European program and of later support of such a program so far as it may be practical for us to do so. The program should be a joint one, agreed to by a number [of], if not all, European nations.

Marshall's proposal linked economic prosperity, democracy, and world peace. In a bold step, the plan suggested that America should take an active role ensuring the interrelated existence of all three, although it was up to the European countries to work together to settle on a unified recovery plan. Even more revolutionary was the fact that, rather than ignore their plight, America's former enemies Germany and Italy were included in the plan. The result of Marshall's proposals was eventually packaged into the European Recovery Program that was passed by Congress in April of 1948.

This act, which pledged $17 billion over four years, soon became known as the Marshall Plan and has been called by this nickname ever since. It was Truman, believing that Marshall deserved more public credit for his military and diplomatic leadership, who insisted on using the name. (Truman also thought that having his name attached to the plan would politicize it during an election year.)

Marshall refused to use the name. He was, however, proud of the purpose of the bill and the effort he put forth for its passage. Traveling across the country during 1947-1948, Marshall likened the intensity of his tour to that of a presidential candidate. Of course, he did not hit the road to promote himself but rather to explain the recovery plan and espouse its merits to the still-isolationist American people and their representatives in Washington, D.C.

Speaking in his typically honest, matter-of-fact, calm manner on January 8, 1948, Marshall said: "This program will cost our country billions of dollars. It will impose a burden on the American taxpayer. It will require sacrifices today in order that we may enjoy security and peace tomorrow."

During September 1947, sixteen European countries and the western occupied zones of Germany submitted

This D. R. Fitzpatrick political cartoon from 1947 is entitled "The Way Back." *(Courtesy of the Granger Collection.)*

their unified proposal for American postwar aid. The cooperation of drawing up a unified plan later helped pave the way for a continent not used to working together to form the North Atlantic Treaty Organization (NATO) and, later, the European Union. Like the Lend-Lease program, the Marshall Plan was a form of eco-

George Marshall was named *Time's* Man of the Year in January of 1947.

nomic diplomacy that rewarded countries whose goals were aligned with those of the United States.

When *Time* named Marshall its Man of the Year (for the second time) in 1947, it said the Marshall Plan "offered hope to those who desperately needed it."

The Marshall Plan was good for the United States in the long run. As part of the four-pronged plan, grants were made to Europeans to buy American goods and services, thus stoking the fires of American commerce by increasing production and exports. The plan encouraged Americans to invest in Europe by guaranteeing that their returns could be obtained in dollars. Investment in Europe was buoyed by the plan's requirement that part of the funds be used to improve European infrastructure. The plan also funded American technical assistance to Europe so that new agricultural and industrial methods could be introduced to the re-modernizing continent.

Although the actual plan was for four years, the Marshall Plan and the philosophy and spirit that it represents has continued to play a significant role in American foreign policy. The U.S. still uses aid to foreign countries to promote democracy, economic stability, and peace.

The Soviets turned down American assistance even though they were invited to participate. In fact, they instituted their own parallel—but ultimately unsuccessful—program of economic assistance called the "Molotov Plan" and pressured the nations they controlled in Central and Eastern Europe to also turn down American aid.

As if to highlight the Soviet menace that the Marshall Plan was partly meant to address, in June 1948 the Soviets blockaded the portion of Berlin that they did not control. By closing highway and railway traffic, the Soviets hoped to squeeze out the Americans, French, and British. To keep West Berlin—a city of 2.5 million people—alive, all necessary supplies were flown in. A minimum of 4,000 tons of food, fuel, and other provisions were needed each day. For nearly a year, American, British, and French fliers airlifted supplies into the besieged city during Operation Vittles. In the end, after 277,264 flights, the Soviets finally allowed land transportation to resume on May 12, 1949. The block-ade was removed and the Cold War continued until the collapse of the So-viet Union in 1991.

Halfway through the Berlin crisis in January of 1949, Marshall again an-nounced his retirement. Though there were still unre-solved global issues, he had accomplished a great deal. He had brought about tremendous change in the State Department, making it a successful and respected Ameri-can institution, and implemented what would come to be known as one of America's most successful diplomatic policies.

George Marshall in 1949. *(Courtesy of the National Portrait Gallery, Smithsonian Institution / Art Resource.)*

TEN

SECRETARY OF DEFENSE

Returning to Dodona, George and Katherine looked forward to retirement. For twenty months, the Marshalls were able to travel, garden, or just sit and talk on the stone patio of their home. Marshall did serve as president of the American Red Cross, doing what might have been considered relatively light work for the charity, meeting with civic leaders to gain their support—yet he still traveled 35,000 miles in a year to fulfill his duties.

In the meantime, while he relaxed, the economic recovery program that bore his name was hard at work. In 1945, France had only 25,000 tractors in its fields, but two years later, thanks to Marshall Plan monies, 100,000 were added. By the end of 1951, Europe's combined gross national products had risen 32.5 percent and European

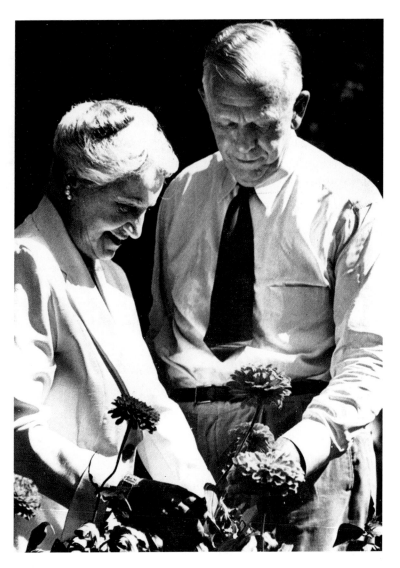

George and Katherine relax together in their garden in 1951. *(Time Life Pictures/Getty Images.)*

industrial production had increased 40 percent over 1938 levels.

In August 1950, George and Katherine were on a fishing vacation at the Huron Mountain resort in Michigan when the former chief of staff and secretary of state was called to a nearby store to take an important call from Washington, D.C. On the phone was President Truman; curious locals heard Marshall say little more than "Yes, Mr. President" before he hung up.

Once again, even though he was almost seventy years old, George C. Marshall was asked to go to work for his country, this time as the secretary of defense. Besides being the principal defense advisor to the president, the job of secretary of defense also meant that Marshall would oversee the enormous Defense Department and formulate and execute military policy. As the new head of the American military, Marshall inherited a very real crisis.

Since the end of WWII hostilities, at public speeches and in private meetings with policy makers, Marshall had regularly preached that America needed to be more thoughtful about its demobilization if it was to live up to the promises it was making to the world, counter the growing Soviet threat, and avoid the frantic buildup prior to both World War I and II. Yet, just as was the case after WWI, America had been only too eager to take itself off a war footing.

Marshall's fears about a lack of manpower were justified when war broke out between American-allied South Korea and Communist North Korea. In August of 1945, the Soviets had invaded the Korean peninsula, then held by Japanese forces. The Soviets encountered little resistance and advanced so quickly that after the war, America proposed dividing the country in two, lest the Soviets come to dominate the whole peninsula. Russia agreed to the partition, splitting Korea at the thirty-eighth parallel, with the Soviets controlling the larger northern section and the Americans controlling the southern, more populous portion. While the initial stated goal of the two sides was to reunite the country, the region became caught up in the conflict between the

The Korean peninsula.

United States and the Soviet Union. For five years following the end of the war, the U.S. was slow to return self-rule to the South while the North, backed by the Soviet Union, continued to push for reunification under its Communist government. Both sides drew up constitutions, each claiming the entire Korean peninsula.

Returning the American-occupied part of Korea to the South Koreans meant entrusting them with defending their own homeland. Except for five hundred military advisors who stayed on, American forces were withdrawn by July of 1949. This left a tiny South Korean military of 53,000 that lacked tanks and had only small arms. The navy only possessed small craft, and the air force—such as it was—consisted of twenty-two training planes.

Kim Il Sung.

North Korean president Kim Il Sung, backed by Soviet premier Joseph Stalin and China's new Communist dictator Mao Tse-tung, attacked South Korea on June 25, 1950, and captured the capital, Seoul, in just three days.

The U.S. dispatched troops to fend off the attack and called on the United Nations, which had been formed after WWII to try to maintain world peace, to follow suit. Sixteen nations came to the aid of South Korea, but it fell to the United States to carry the brunt of the work. America, however, had demobilized its WWII army and lacked adequate forces to meet the challenge.

The military lack of preparedness is what brought Marshall back from retirement. The Korean War threatened to spill over into a fight with China or Russia. The best man to raise an army and run a war was George Marshall. Feeling his age, Marshall agreed to take the position as secretary of defense for only six months (though he would actually stay for a whole year). He said, ruefully, "I was getting rather hardened to coming in when everything had gone to pot . . . and darned if I didn't find the same thing when I came into the Korean War."

On top of everything else, Truman also hoped Marshall could repair the fractured relationship between the State Department and the Defense Department, which was largely the result of incompatible personalities at the top of the two organizations. In this respect, Marshall was uniquely qualified. Aside from being almost universally admired, he knew the top officials of both departments very well.

Once again Marshall oversaw a draft to bulk up the army. And he was again brought into conflict with MacArthur, who was leading the army in Korea under the banner of the United Nations. Initially, this intervention abroad against Communist influence saw public approval ratings of nearly 70 percent. However, as casualties mounted and the war dragged on, approval ratings slipped to 40 and 30 percent.

After a tremendous counteroffensive to drive the invading North Koreans from South Korea, MacArthur pressed on to capture Pyongyang, the capital of North Korea. He then advanced to the Chinese border and eventually, against orders from Washington, D.C., proceeded to provoke the Chinese. MacArthur was convinced he could defeat the Communist Chinese. His assumption proved incorrect; the United Nations forces suffered a defeat that required MacArthur to pull back.

Although he was a celebrated commander whose abilities were well recognized, MacArthur's decision to press the attack was motivated by personal glory and an unfailing belief in his own strategy rather than the military and diplomatic considerations of his superiors. He took exception to both American and United Nations directives and criticized how his superiors were running what was being called a "police action" rather than an open war. MacArthur insisted that the fight should be taken to the Chinese on their home soil. With respect to international reluctance to start a war with China, he famously declared that "there was no substitute for victory."

As a result of his insubordination, Truman insisted that MacArthur be relieved of his command. Secretary of Defense Marshall and other military leaders, however, were hesitant to remove the revered general. In the end, the order was put through, and MacArthur was stripped of his duties in Korea on April 11, 1951—to his immense displeasure.

The incident produced a backlash among the American people and legislators who respected the almost mythic MacArthur. Marshall and Truman suffered savage attacks because of the personal insult to MacArthur and because of their decision not to press for war with Communist China, which made it appear that the United States was not wholly committed to preventing the spread of communism. Among the many critics of the move was Republican senator Joseph McCarthy, who seized on the opportunity to brand the Democratic administration as pro-Communist. On June 14, McCarthy unleashed a three-hour diatribe against Marshall on the

Senator Joseph McCarthy.

Senate floor. The comments, which ran to 60,000 words, were widely circulated and eventually published as *America's Retreat from Victory: The Story of George Catlett Marshall.*

Time magazine said that "McCarthy twisted quotes" and "drew unwarranted conclusions from the facts he did get right." Although most of McCarthy's fellow senators tired of the attack—it was reported that of the few who showed up for the reading, most walked out and only two remained until the end—it did leave a mark on Marshall and hastened his desire to retire again. In the end, congressional hearings were held. After listening to testimony, a committee found that relieving MacArthur was warranted. Years later, Truman said of his action, "I fired him because he wouldn't respect the authority of the President." General Bradley was more to the point when he said MacArthur wanted to involve America "in the wrong war, at the wrong place, at the wrong time and with the wrong enemy."

Never one for pomp and circumstance, Marshall walked into a staff meeting on one September morning in 1951 and casually said, "At eleven o'clock I cease to be Secretary of Defense." He had complained that a new crisis was always arising and there was never a good time to leave, but his latest mission of preparing the military and mending the fences between the State and Defense departments had been accomplished. Marshall retired for the final time.

Retreating to Dodona, Marshall saw Dwight D.

Eisenhower, the soldier whom he had often treated like a son, elected president of the United States. Marshall was content to observe events from afar, even turning down a reported $1 million offer to write his memoirs.

In 1953, Eisenhower asked Marshall to head the American delegation to the coronation of England's Queen Elizabeth II. Though he had been sent to pay America's respects to the new sovereign, the tables were turned on Marshall. In Westminster Abbey, Winston Churchill stepped out of the procession to shake Marshall's hand. Following the former prime minister's lead, other British dignitaries did the same. As Marshall walked back to take his seat, the vast audience stood. Wondering who should deserve such a dramatic show of unified respect, Marshall looked around, confused, only to realize that it was for him. Grateful Britons had not forgotten his efforts to save their country and their continent, both as a military commander and as the architect of the Marshall Plan.

Marshall was again thrust into the global spotlight upon receiving word that he had won the prestigious Nobel Peace Prize for his work in bringing peace and prosperity to postwar Europe through the Marshall Plan.

After being notified of the award, Marshall characteristically deflected any personal glory and dedicated the prize to the American people: "While the award is individual in nature, it is, in effect, a tribute to the American people for their unselfish devotion to the welfare of free people everywhere."

Marshall traveled to Oslo, Norway, to accept the Nobel. Speaking at the awards ceremony, Marshall explained: "There has been considerable comment over the awarding of the Nobel Peace Prize to a soldier. I am afraid this does not seem as remarkable to me as it quite evidently appears to others. I know a great deal of the horrors and tragedies of war. . . . The cost of war in human lives is constantly spread before me, written neatly in many ledgers whose columns are gravestones. I am deeply moved to find some means or method of avoiding another calamity of war."

Marshall receiving the Nobel Peace Prize in Oslo, Norway, on December 10, 1953. *(World Wide Photos)*

Though the award was given for his postwar actions, Marshall's speech focused on eliminating the causes of war, highlighting a three-pronged approach. First, more emphasis must be placed on educating the world's citizens about the causes of war in a scientific and unbiased manner using objective facts rather than national biases. Second, Marshall expressed hope for better international understanding of different peoples and cultures. He recalled how he was able to interact with the French peasantry during his time in World War I, and that such cultural exchanges helped foster a global sense of togetherness and cooperation. Finally, Marshall advocated eliminating poverty and the root causes that lead to the creation of tyrannies. "Tyranny inevitably must retire before the tremendous moral strength of the gospel of freedom and self-respect for the individual, but we have to recognize that these democratic principles do not flourish on empty stomachs, and that people turn to false promises of dictators because they are hopeless and anything promises something better than the miserable existence that they endure."

Returning from Europe, Marshall's health began to decline. He made several trips to the hospital, fighting off the flu and pneumonia. A stroke early in 1959 put him in a wheelchair, and he was soon afflicted by brain spasms that further weakened his faculties. When Eisenhower and Churchill visited him at Walter Reed Army Hospital, he was unable to recognize them.

On October 16, 1959, George C. Marshall died. The man who had so influenced America's place in the world—in

WWI, WWII, as secretary of state and of defense—deserved the sort of send-off reserved for great statesman and military heroes. Roosevelt's funeral cortège had included a black draped caisson drawn by six white horses, along with full military honors, and Pershing and MacArthur saw similar tributes upon their deaths. In a final testament to his strongly held beliefs that one should not be idolized for doing one's job, Marshall explicitly requested of his wife that his funeral be small and private. He instructed: "Bury me simply, like any ordinary officer of the U.S. Army who has served his country honorably. No fuss. No elaborate ceremonials. Keep the service short, confine the guest-list to the family. And above everything, do it quietly." For the most part, Katherine Marshall acquiesced, though the family-only rule was broken to allow both President Eisenhower and former President Truman to attend.

Having served nine presidents, Marshall bridged the gap in America's transition from a nation with fresh memories of the Civil War to a superpower that dominated world affairs. He had gone from a struggling student who commanded a few hundred fellow cadets to overseeing millions of men during the world's largest conflict. In his tenure as soldier and statesman, George Marshall defined the American Century.

Of him, Truman said, "He was the greatest general since Robert E. Lee. He was the greatest administrator since Thomas Jefferson. He was the man of honor, the man of truth, the man of greatest ability. He was the greatest of the great of our time."

TIMELINE

1880   George Catlett Marshall Jr. was born in
            Uniontown, Pennsylvania, on December 31.
1897-1901   Studies at Virginia Military Institute.
1902   Marries Elizabeth "Lily" Carter Coles and re-
            ceives army commission as second lieutenant.
1902-1903   Serves in the Philippines.
1906-1910   Studies and then instructs at Fort Leavenworth.
1913-1916   Second tour in the Philippines.
1917-1919   Serves in World War I with the First Division
            and at General Pershing's headquarters.
1924-1927   Serves with Fifteenth Infantry Regiment in
            China; Elizabeth Marshall dies in September
            1927; becomes assistant commandant at Fort
            Benning in October.
1930   Marries Katherine Boyce Tupper Brown.
1932-1933   Commands posts and CCC camps at Fort Screven
            and Fort Moultrie.
1933-1936   Serves as senior instructor with the Illinois
            National Guard.
1936   Promoted to brigadier general and given com-
            mand of Vancouver Barracks in Washington
            state.

1939	Officially named chief of staff; World War II begins on the same day, September 1.
1941	Surprise attack on Pearl Harbor, December 7.
1944	Eisenhower commands massive D-Day invasion starting June 6.
1945	Atomic bombs dropped on Japan in August, effectively ending World War II.
1945	Marshall retires as chief of staff; sent to China as an ambassador.
1947-1949	Serves as secretary of state; oversees the Marshall Plan and the Berlin airlift.
1950-1951	Serves as secretary of defense.
1953	Wins Nobel Peace Prize.
1959	Dies at Walter Reed Army Hospital on October 16; buried in plain grave at Arlington National Cemetery.

SOURCES

CHAPTER ONE: From Uniontown to VMI

p. 14, "My father was so . . ." Forrest C. Pogue, *George C. Marshall, Education of a General* (New York: Viking, 1963), 5.

p. 16-17, "I told her . . ." George C. Marshall, *Interviews and Reminiscences,* interviewed by Forrest C. Pogue, George C. Marshall Foundation, http://www.marshallfoundation.org/ chpt1-2.pdf (accessed 3/17/05).

p. 17-18, "He was trying . . ." Leonard Mosely, *Marshall: Hero For Our Times* (New York: Hearst Books, 1982), 10.

p. 19, "It was part of . . ." Pogue, *Education,* 44.

p. 22, "What I learned . . ." Ibid., 46.

p. 22, "would judge you . . ." Ibid., 54.

p. 23, "I intend to . . ." Ibid., 56.

p. 23, "I was much . . ." Ed Cray, *General of the Army George C. Marshall, Soldier and Statesman* (New York: W. W. Norton & Company, 1990), 29.

CHAPTER TWO: Brilliant Young Officer

p. 26, "If commissioned in . . ." Pogue, *Education,* 63.

p. 26-27, "I had no appointment . . ." Ibid., 64-65.

p. 30, "I am not exaggerating . . ." Ibid., 72.

p. 31, "the hardest service . . ." Mark A. Stoler, *George C. Marshall: Solider-Statesman of the American Century* (Boston: Twayne Publishers, 1989), 17.

p. 31, "the best one . . ." Pogue, *Education,* 89.

p. 33, "I finally got into . . ." Ibid., 96.

p. 36, "I had an opportunity . . ." Stoler, *George C. Marshall,* 26.

p. 38, "Japanese officers . . ." Pogue, *Education,* 124-125.

p. 39, "The absolute stagnation . . ." Ibid., 129-130.

CHAPTER THREE: Preparations

p. 47, "I saw more . . ." Mosley, *Marshall,* 45.

p. 47, "You fellows came down . . ." Ibid., 46.

p. 48, "Yes, but I . . . and the nation," Pogue, *Education,* 138.

p. 48, "The army and . . ." Stoler, *George C. Marshall,* 27-28.

CHAPTER FOUR: World War I

p. 52, "If the French . . ." Center of Military History, United States Army, *United States Army in the World War 1917-1919—Training and Use of American Units with the British and French Volume 3* (Washington, D.C.: United States Army, 1948), 238.

p. 54, "General Pershing, there's . . . solved before night," Mosely, *Marshall,* 59.

p. 56-57, "I doubt that . . ." Pogue, *Education,* 168.

p. 57, "He could hardly . . ." William Manchester, *American Caesar* (Boston: Little, Brown and Company, 1978), 89.

p. 64, "My mother was . . ." Stoler, *George C. Marshall,* 110.

p. 65, "My five years . . ." Pogue, *Education,* 226.

CHAPTER FIVE: New Beginnings

p. 70, "an unlimited field . . ." Pogue, *Education,* 248.

p. 74, "I found it was . . ." Ibid., 254.

p. 77, "Rather dilapidated after . . ." Katherine Tupper Marshall, *Together: Annals of an Army Wife* (New York: Tupper and Love, 1946), 10.

p. 78, "However small . . ." Pogue, *Education,* 272.

p. 79-80, "I deplore the fact . . ." Ibid., 285.

p. 80, "He has no superior . . ." Ibid., 282.

p. 81, "had a grey . . ." Marshall, *Together,* 18.

p. 82, "A welcome from . . ." Ibid., 23-24.

CHAPTER SIX: Chief of Staff

p. 89, "I think you . . ." Stoler, *George C. Marshall,* 68.

p. 89, "You said yes . . ." Pogue, *Education,* 330.

p. 90-91, "On July 1, 1939 . . ." George C. Marshall, *The War Reports of General of the Army George C. Marshall Chief of Staff, General of the Army H. H. Arnold Commanding General, Army Air Forces, Fleet Admiral Ernest J. King, Commander-in-Chief, United States Fleet and Chief of Naval Operations* (New York: J. B. Lippincott Company, 1947), 16.

p. 92, "I know exactly . . ." Forrest C. Pogue, *George C. Marshall: Ordeal and Hope* (New York: Viking, 1965), 30.

p. 93, "If you don't . . ." Ibid., 31.

p. 96, "Get these blankets . . ." Ibid., 109.

p. 96, "Take a method . . ." Nathan Miller, *F. D. R.: An Intimate History* (New York: Doubleday and Co., 1983), 263.

p. 98, "I want the mistake . . ." Pogue, *Ordeal and Hope,* 89.

p. 102-103, "Some of our people . . ." "Franklin D. Roosevelt, On National Security," Franklin Delano Roosevelt Library and Museum, http://www.fdrlibrary.marist.edu/122940.html (accessed 3/17/05).

CHAPTER SEVEN: War

p. 106-107, "Chances of favorable . . ." Cray, *General of the Army,* 240-241.

p. 107, "Negotiations with Japanese . . ." Mosely, *Marshall,* 165.

p. 110, "Yesterday, December 7 . . ." Franklin D. Roosevelt, "Address to Congress Requesting a Declaration of War with Japan December 8, 1941," Franklin D. Roosevelt Library and Museum, http://www.fdrlibrary.marist.edu/tmirhdee.html (accessed 3/18/05).

p. 110, "The long known . . ." Franklin D. Roosevelt, "To the Congress of the United States," Franklin D. Roosevelt Library and Museum, http://www.fdrlibrary.marist.edu/andyc/fdr/psf/box1/t07m01.html (accessed 3/18/05).

p. 115, "always in a rage," Stoler, *George C. Marshall,* 117.

p. 115, "We can't afford . . ." Ibid.

p. 116, "I am convinced . . ." Pogue, *Ordeal and Hope,* 276.

CHAPTER EIGHT: Operation Overlord

p. 123, "the Pershing of WWII," Mary Sutton Skutt and Rachel Yarnell Thompson, *America's Hero to the World, George C. Marshall* (Leesburg, VA: The George C. Marshall International Center, 1999), 83.

p. 123, "Ike, you and . . ." Forrest C. Pogue, *George C. Marshall: Organizer of Victory* (New York: Viking, 1973), 303.

p. 123, "the suggested transfer . . ." Ibid., 272.

p. 124, "I just repeated . . ." Ibid., 321.

p. 124-125, "You know I do . . ." Skutt, *America's Hero,* 84.

p. 130, "We had to . . ." Mosely, *Marshall,* 338.

p. 131, "In a war . . ." Stoler, *George C. Marshall,* 142.

p. 131, "organizer of victory," Pogue, *Organizer of Victory,* 585.

CHAPTER NINE: Cold War

p. 132, "From Stettin in . . ." Winston Churchill, "Iron Curtain Speech," National Center for Public Policy Research, http://www.nationalcenter.org/ChurchillIronCurtain.html (accessed 3/18/05).

p. 133, "My retirement was . . ." Stoler, *George C. Marshall,* 145.

p. 136, "My battle out . . ." Ibid., 150.

p. 139, "I think for . . ." Forrest C. Pogue, *George C. Marshall: Statesman* (New York: Viking, 1987), 147.

p. 142, "I believe that . . ." Harry S. Truman, "Special Message to the Congress on Greece and Turkey: The Truman Doctrine," The Harry S.Truman Library and Museum, http://www.trumanlibrary.org/publicpapers/index.php?pid=2189 (accessed 3/18/05).

p. 142-144, "The truth of the . . ." Charles L. Mee Jr., *The Marshall Plan: The Launching of the Pax Americana* (New York: Simon and Schuster, 1984), 272-273.

p. 145, "This program will . . ." Cray, *General of the Army,* 621.

p. 147, "offered hope to . . ." Pogue, *Statesman,* 237.

CHAPTER TEN: Secretary of Defense

p. 152, "Yes, Mr. President," Ibid., 420.

p. 155, "I was getting . . ." Stoler, *George C. Marshall,* 183.

p. 156, "there was no . . ." Pogue, *Statesman,* 481.

p. 158, "McCarthy twisted . . . get right." Ibid., 489.

p. 158, "I fired him . . ." Stoler, *George C. Marshall,* 186-187.

p. 158, "in the wrong . . ." Ibid., 188-189.

p. 158, "At eleven o'clock . . ." Pogue, *Statesman,* 491.

p. 159, "While the award . . ." Ibid., 504.

p. 160, "There has been . . ." Nobel Web Site, www.nobel.se/peace/laureates/1953/marshall-lecture.html#not1

p. 161, "Tyranny inevitably must . . ." Ibid.

p. 162, "Bury me simply . . ." Mosley, *Marshall,* 523.

p. 162, "He was the . . ." "Marshall Buried After Simple Rite," *New York Times*, October 21, 1959, p. 3.

BIBLIOGRAPHY

Baldwin, Hanson W. "Big Forces Are Massed For Showdown in Pacific." *The New York Times*. December 7, 1941, p. 4E.

Beal, John Robinson. *Marshall in China*. Garden City: Doubleday & Company, 1970.

Center of Military History, United States Army. *United States Army in the World War 1917-1919—Training and Use of American Units with the British and French Volume 3*. Washington, D.C.: United States Army, 1948.

Churchill, Winston. "Iron Curtain Speech." National Center for Public Policy Research. http://www.nationalcenter.org/ChurchillIronCurtain.html.

Cole, Wayne S. *America First: The Battle Against Intervention: 1940-1941*. Madison: The University of Wisconsin Press, 1953.

Cray, Ed. *General of the Army: George C. Marshall, Soldier and Statesman*. New York: W.W. Norton & Company, 1990.

Dear, I. C. B., ed. *The Oxford Companion to World War II*. New York: Oxford University Press, 1995.

Dedijer, Vladimir. *The Road to Sarajevo*. New York: Simon and Schuster, 1966.

Faber, Harold. *Soldier and Statesman: General George C. Marshall*. New York: Ariel Books, 1964.

Ferrell, Robert H. *The American Secretaries of State and Their Diplomacy: Volume XV: George C. Marshall as Secretary of State, 1947-1949*. New York: Cooper Square Publishers, 1966.

"German Army Attacks Poland; Cities Bombed, Port Blockaded; Danzig Is Accepted …" *New York Times*, September 1, 1939.

Hansen, Arthur A., ed. *Japanese American World War II Evacuation Oral History Project: Part I: Internees.* Westport: Meckler, 1991.

Heyman, Neil M. *World War I.* Westport: Greenwood Press, 1997.

Huntington, Samuel P. *The Soldier and the State: The Theory and Politics of Civil-Military Relations.* New York: Vintage Books, 1957.

"Joint Plans to Thwart Japan." *New York Times.* December 7, 1941.

Larrabee, Eric. *Commander in Chief: Franklin Delano Roosevelt, His Lieutenants and Their War.* New York: Simon & Schuster, 1987.

MacArthur, Brian, ed. *The Penguin Book of Twentieth Century Speeches.* London: Viking, 1992.

MacArthur, Douglas. *Reminiscences.* New York: McGraw-Hill Book Company, 1964.

Manchester, William. *American Caesar.* Boston: Little, Brown and Company, 1978.

"Marshall Buried After Simple Rite." *New York Times*, October 21, 1959.

Marshall, George C. "Essentials to Peace." Nobelprize.org. http://www.nobel.se/peace/laureates/1953/marshall-lecture.html#not1.

———. *Memoirs of My Services in the World War: 1917-1918.* Boston: Houghton Mifflin Company, 1976.

———, H. H. Arnold, and Ernest J. King. *The War Reports of General of the Army George C. Marshall Chief of staff, General of the Army H. H. Arnold Commanding General, Army Air Forces, Fleet Admiral Ernest J. King, Commander-In-Chief, United States Fleet and Chief of Naval Operations.* Philadelphia: J.B. Lippincott Company, 1947.

Marshall, Katherine Tupper. *Together: Annals of an Army Wife.* New York: Tupper and Love, 1946.

Mee, Charles L., Jr. *The Marshall Plan: The Launching of the Pax Americana.* New York: Simon and Schuster, 1984.

Miller, Nathan. *F. D. R..: An Intimate History.* New York: Doubleday and Co., 1983.

Mosley, Leonard. *Marshall: Hero For Our Times.* New York: Hearst Books, 1982.

Morgan, Ted. *FDR: A Biography.* New York: Simon and Schuster, 1985.

Pogue, Forrest C. *George C. Marshall: Education of a General.* New York: Viking, 1963.

———. *George C. Marshall: Ordeal and Hope.* New York: Viking, 1965.

———. *George C. Marshall: Organizer of Victory.* New York: Viking, 1973.

———. *George C. Marshall: Statesman.* New York: Viking, 1987.

Roosevelt, Franklin D. "On National Security." Franklin D. Roosevelt Presidential Library and Museum. http://www.fdrlibrary.marist.edu/122940.html.

Skutt, Mary Sutton and Rachel Yarnell Thompson. *America's Hero to the World, George C. Marshall.* Leesburg: The George C. Marshall International Center, 1999.

Stoler, Mark A. *George C. Marshall: Soldier-Statesman of the American Century.* Boston: Twayne Publishers, 1989.

Truman, Harry S. "Special Message to the Congress on Greece and Turkey: The Truman Doctrine." Harry S. Truman Library & Museum. http://www.trumanlibrary.org/publicpapers/index.php?pid=2189.

Wilson, Rose Page. *General Marshall Remembered.* Englewood Cliffs: Prentice-Hall, 1968.

Winter, J.M. *The Experience of World War I.* New York: Oxford University Press, 1989.

WEB SITES

http://www.marshallfoundation.org/
The George C. Marshall Foundation keeps the general's legacy
of service alive, offering information, educational materials,
and even scholarships.

http://nobelprize.org/peace/laureates/1953/marshall-bio.html
An online biography of Marshall, with a link to his complete
Nobel Prize acceptance speech.

http://www.npg.si.edu/exh/marshall/
An exhibit at the National Portrait Gallery devoted to Marshall,
with lots of photographs online.

http://www.loc.gov/exhibits/marshall/
A Library of Congress exhibit celebrating the fiftieth anniver-
sary of the Marshall Plan.

http://www.pbs.org/wgbh/amex/macarthur/
An online complement to the PBS film "MacArthur," complete
with transcripts, images, educational resources, and more.

INDEX